Zeenath Reza Khan. Pradnya Bhagwat. Patrick Mukala. Nkqubela Ruxwana
Editors

Future-Proofing Businesses Through Smart *IS* and Emerging Technologies

Your guide to understanding SME pain points and leveraging digital innovation for growth, resilience, and sustainability

UNIVERSITY
OF WOLLONGONG
IN DUBAI

CENTRE FOR
ACADEMIC INTEGRITY
IN THE UAE

European Network
for Academic Integrity
Outreach Working Group

GULF BOOK
SERVICES

Editors

Zeenath Reza Khan
School of Computer Science
University of Wollongong in
Dubai

Pradnya Bhagwat
School of Computer Science
University of Wollongong in
Dubai

Patrick Mukala
School of Computer Science
University of Wollongong in
Dubai

Nkqubela Ruxwana
School of Computer Science
University of Wollongong in
Dubai

Copyright & Publishing Information

Cover Design
Marwan Trading LLC, United Arab Emirates

Book Design and Typesetting
Ing. Veronika Krasnican, European Network for Academic Integrity

Availability
This book is published in an open-access spirit and is made globally available through Amazon for a nominal server charge of USD 1, to ensure broad accessibility and sustainable distribution.

ISBN: 978-1-917529-28-0
Year: November 2025
Typeset in Garamond

Special Note from Director of Research, University of Wollongong in Dubai

In a time of rapid and often disruptive technological change, with artificial intelligence and related innovations reshaping industries, significant opportunities are opening for companies to harness technology in support of their strategic needs. This book explores how technology, and in particular smart information systems and emerging technologies, can be applied to address challenges faced by real-world businesses in the sustainability sector in the United Arab Emirates.

I am deeply grateful for the generous response we have received from industry partners who shared their pressing challenges with us, and for their willingness to engage in collaborative solutions. Their openness has enabled a dialogue between academia and practice that lies at the heart of meaningful innovation. I am equally proud of the dedication and creativity shown by students and staff at the University of Wollongong in Dubai. Their commitment to applying technological knowledge to complex business problems illustrates the vital role that higher education can play in shaping a more responsible future.

The first responsibility of any university is to serve its local community. The chapters in this volume demonstrate how universities can generate impact within their cities and regions, not only by producing ideas and research, but by translating them into proposed practice. Through innovation, experimentation, and practical implementation in small and medium-sized enterprises, universities can help to future-proof businesses, strengthen resilience, and support the wider transition to sustainable development.

I hope that readers will find in these pages both inspiration and concrete examples of how technology, thoughtfully applied, can help sustainable businesses thrive as they face that challenges of tomorrow.

Dr Stephen Wilkinson
Director of Research
University of Wollongong in Dubai
Dubai, UAE

Special Note from a University of Wollongong in Dubai Alum

When we start something new, we always look around to seek guidance, advice and a helping hand to accelerate and make progress faster. This is most true when starting life after graduating from university, or being a startup, where there is lots of uncertainty, pressure, and the desire to succeed.

We look to those who have done things before us to take help and find our way in the complex corporate world. Those of us who are lucky to have had success throughout a long career carry a great responsibility, and opportunity to add value back to the ecosystem they came through. Many students who graduate out of university with passion, energy, and motivation have little guidance and mentorship available from industry experts. As they are offered the right mentors, the right connections, they do wonders with technology, problem solving and find innovative ways to achieve success.

Alumni of universities are key to deliver this value and nurture those who follow the same path their predecessors did. Alumni can help them avoid mistakes, find the right avenues and ensure that in return they deliver success for themselves and their mentors.

Mr. Muhammad Hamad
Alum, UOWD
Manager - Service Performance
Help AG UAE

Foreword

When I graduated college in 1998, the world was amid the dot-com boom. I began my career as a web developer, watching businesses scramble to build an online presence, and later shifted into academia to research, teach, and write about e-commerce. That wave of innovation reshaped entire industries and redefined how society interacts with technology. But what I witnessed then pales in comparison to the transformation we are experiencing now. Artificial intelligence and other smart technologies are spreading faster, attracting far greater investment, and generating revenue at a scale the Internet could only dream of in its early years. OpenAI alone has grown its revenue nearly tenfold in just two years, and the global AI industry is forecast to expand 30–40% annually for the next five years. For organizations, the imperative is clear: adapt or be left behind. Yet small and medium enterprises, unlike large corporations, often lack the knowledge and resources to manage such radical change, leaving them at risk of missing the most important technological shift of our time.

"Future-Proofing Businesses Through Smart IS and Emerging Technologies" provides a basis for that knowledge. In a series of eight chapters authored by students and faculty at the University of Wollongong in Dubai, the book captures key lessons on transformations of SME in the United Arab Emirates (UAE). These lessons support the strategic goals of the UAE to become a regional power in digital transformation, as articulated in their AI Strategy 2031. This book provides practical and timely guidance to SMEs to align with this national strategy.

The chapters highlight three cross-cutting themes: the need to integrate existing technologies before introducing new innovations; the importance of measuring sustainability with clear, quantifiable metrics; and the role of partnerships in accelerating growth within the UAE SME ecosystem. These themes echo lessons from around the world, such as in my textbook on e-commerce which includes sections on technology integration, SMART goals, and strategic partnerships. However, this book concretizes these themes within UAE.

Under the capable hands of Dr. Zeenath Khan, et. al, the chapters were edited for this book. Dr. Khan's work in academic integrity at the Centre for Academic Integrity in the UAE shows her passion for training and preparing students, teachers, and policy makers in ethical foundations necessary for using smart technologies effectively. Using students to author chapters prepares them for thoughtful and practical approaches to learning. Through this approach, students gain a platform for creating impactful work while simultaneously learning deep personal lessons, blending teaching and research. Few experiences are more gratifying as a professor than learning that a student's writing has been accepted for publication.

In the pages ahead, you will journey through a series of business cases with critical lessons for SMEs to consider. I believe these lessons will inspire executives and entrepreneurs on how to future proof their organizations with the coming wave of smart technologies. I invite you to learn from these talented students and to embrace the playbook for transformative change.

Dr John R. Drake
Professor of Management Information System, East Carolina University
Author of E-Commerce: A Stakeholder Approach
Greenville, NC, USA

Preface

As educators, we have always believed that learning must extend beyond the classroom. True education happens when students are immersed in real-world challenges, empowered to experiment, and encouraged to connect their knowledge with practical solutions. This playbook reflects that philosophy.

Our passion lies in engaging students in work-integrated learning, creating opportunities for them to step into the shoes of innovators, problem-solvers, and changemakers. Over the years, we have seen how powerful this approach becomes when alumni, industry partners, and the wider community rally behind it. Through corporate social responsibility (CSR) initiatives, mentorship, and collaborations, our students are given platforms to shine, while industry gains fresh insights that are unconstrained by legacy thinking.

We firmly believe that students are not only the future of the workforce but also its most creative architects. They are naturally tech-savvy, quick to adapt, and fearless when it comes to thinking outside the box. They bring with them a worldview that is unfiltered, imaginative, and deeply engaged with both technology and society. What better way, then, to showcase their potential than by asking them to tackle the pressing pain points of SMEs and propose solutions rooted in their vision of the future?

Each chapter in this playbook has been authored by students from Information Systems courses. Working with SME cases from across the UAE, they have designed digital transformation strategies that are grounded in the realities of business but also inspired by the possibilities of technology. Their voices are present in every page - young, bold, and insightful.

This preface is, therefore, both an invitation and a celebration. It invites readers to see through the eyes of the next generation of innovators and reminds us that when given the right platform, students can contribute meaningfully to national priorities such as digital transformation, sustainability, and entrepreneurship. And it celebrates the courage, creativity, and commitment of our students who, in taking on these challenges, have shown that the future is not something we must wait for, it is something they are already building.

Dr Zeenath Reza Khan
Ms Pradnya Bhagwat
Dr Patrick Mukala
Dr Nkqubela Ruxwana

Table of Contents

INTRODUCTION   13
Zeenath Reza Khan . Pradnya Bhagwat . Patrick Mukala . Nkqubela Ruxwana

SECTION I - OPERATIONS-FIRST APPROACH

CHAPTER 1   27
Empowering Sustainable Growth with Smart IS: A Fashion SME
Experience
Asraa Noohu Shaikh . Advaith Sujith . Rhythm Shahi Bikram . Anushka Roy

CHAPTER 2   41
Intelligent & Sustainable Supply Chain for Smart Retail
Ashton Vivian Tauro . Abel Varughese . Aagna Samhita Sapavat . Loulieh Arar

SECTION II - MARKET-FIRST APPROACH

CHAPTER 3   59
Building a Conscious Commerce Engine: A Smart IS Framework for a
UAE-based eco-friendly fashion marketplace
Taha Shabbir Hussain . Akhil Anil Kumar . Maryam Elgamil

SECTION III - CUSTOMER-FIRST APPROACH

CHAPTER 4   79
Next-Gen CRMs for SMEs: Enhancing Customer Engagement with RAP
Plugins
Nigel Noronha . Raphael Dypiangco . Frenica D'souza . Nathan Matthew

CHAPTER 5   95
Enabling Business Intelligence through Unified CRM Ecosystems
Sara Ranjbar. Farhana Islam . Hawra Virani

SECTION IV - SYNTHESIS

CHAPTER 6   109
Connecting the Dots: Innovation, Entrepreneurship, and the Sustainable
Future
Marouane Khallouk

11

CONCLUSION 123

Advancing Smart IS Adoption for UAE SMEs: Conclusion, Reflections, and Recommendations

Patrick Mukala . Nkqubela Ruxwana . Zeenath Reza Khan . Pradnya Bhagwat

ACKNOWLEDGEMENTS 143

DECLARATIONS 144

Introduction

From Fragmentation to Integration – Future-Proofing UAE SMEs through Smart Information Systems

Zeenath Reza Khan . Pradnya Bhagwat . Patrick Mukala . Nkqubela Ruxwana

Abstract
In this introductory chapter, we set the stage for understanding how small and medium enterprises (SMEs) in the UAE can transform fragmentation into integration through smart information systems. Drawing on national strategies such as *We the UAE 2031* and the UAE Digital Economy Strategy, the chapter highlights how technology adoption is no longer optional but essential for competitiveness. It explores the pressures SMEs face, from customer expectations of instant digital service to accountability under Net Zero 2050, while positioning cloud CRMs, AI-driven analytics, and IoT-enabled supply chains as enablers of resilience and sustainability. Most importantly, this chapter introduces the playbook's unique approach: student-authored cases that blend academic rigor with practical SME realities. Together, they provide a roadmap for future-proofing SMEs through integration, innovation, and measurable impact.

Keywords
SMEs, digital transformation, smart information systems, sustainability, UAE Vision 2031

Zeenath Reza Khan ✉
University of Wollongong in Dubai
zeenathkhan@uowdubai.ac.ae

Pradnya Bhagwat
University of Wollongong in Dubai

Patrick Mukala
University of Wollongong in Dubai

Nkqubela Ruxwana
University of Wollongong in Dubai

Khan, Z. R., Bhagwat, P., Mukala, P., & Ruxwana, N. (2025). From fragmentation to integration: Future-proofing UAE SMEs through smart information systems. In Z. R. Khan, P. Bhagwat, P. Mukala, & N. Ruxwana (Eds.), *Technology adoption playbook for sustainability-focused startups and SMEs* (pp. 13-23). ENAI WG Centre for Academic Integrity in the UAE; University of Wollongong in Dubai; Gulf Book Services LTD, UK.

1. SMEs, Smart IS, and the UAE Vision

Small and medium-sized enterprises (SMEs) are not only the backbone of the UAE economy but also a central pillar of the nation's aspirations for a diversified, innovation-driven future. Representing more than 94 percent of registered companies, SMEs contribute significantly to employment, GDP, and social mobility (Shrivastava and Riaz, 2023), with the UAE Government noting that over 557,000 SMEs contribute around 63.5 percent to the nation's non-oil GDP (IFZA, 2023; WUAB, 2023). Yet, their survival and growth are increasingly challenged by fragmented systems, inefficient processes, and the rising expectations of customers in a hyper-digital age.

The UAE government has placed SMEs at the heart of its economic agenda. The national strategy, *We the UAE 2031*, outlines an ambitious goal of doubling GDP to AED 3 trillion and achieving AED 800 billion in non-oil exports, with SMEs contributing nearly 60 percent to this expansion (UAE Government Portal, 2024). Complementing this vision, the UAE Digital Economy Strategy seeks to double the contribution of the digital economy to GDP within a decade (UAE Government Portal, 2022), while positioning the nation as a global leader in technological adoption and entrepreneurship. Within this framework, SMEs are expected not only to compete but also to innovate and align with sustainability imperatives.

Smart information systems (IS), including cloud-based CRMs, AI-driven analytics, IoT-enabled supply chains, and integrated business intelligence platforms, provide the key to bridging the gap between ambition and execution. For SMEs constrained by limited resources, such tools offer scalable, modular solutions that unify fragmented data, streamline operations, and create measurable sustainability impact. The integration of these technologies is not just about efficiency; it is about building resilience and trust in markets that demand speed, transparency, and responsibility.

It is important to note that the chapters in this playbook are authored by students from the University of Wollongong in Dubai (UOWD)'s Information Systems courses. Based on illustrative SME scenarios developed through work-integrated projects across the UAE, these students developed practical, technology-driven proposed solutions that reflect both academic rigor and entrepreneurial realities. Their contributions illustrate the power of experiential learning in higher education, where classroom knowledge is applied directly to industry challenges. As editors, we view this playbook not just as an academic resource, but as evidence of how education, entrepreneurship, and innovation can intersect to shape the future of SMEs.

2. The SME Digital-Sustainability Nexus

Across industries, SMEs face recurring pain points: scattered data, sluggish customer responses, manual onboarding, unreliable forecasting, and difficulty in quantifying sustainability commitments Steidle et al., 2025). These weaknesses are not unique to the UAE, but the local context magnifies them. Mobile-first consumers in the UAE increasingly demand near-instant service, with 67% reporting that their most recent retail purchase was made via smartphone (Gulf Today, 2025; Pearl Digital, 2025). Fast-moving logistics raise expectations for same-day or next-day fulfilment, with providers in Dubai and Abu Dhabi rapidly scaling last-mile delivery solutions (Nexdigm, 2025; Harmon, 2025). At the same time, national sustainability goals such as UAE Net Zero 2050 hold companies accountable for measurable environmental action, pushing logistics and e-commerce providers toward green delivery practices (Harmon, 2025; Liamzon, 2024).

Smart IS provides a lens through which to reimagine SME competitiveness. Integration sits at the heart of this transformation. By unifying customer data, operational workflows, and sustainability tracking into a single digital backbone, SMEs can build capabilities that extend beyond survival to scalable growth. This mirrors the dynamic capabilities framework in management research: firms succeed not by static assets but by their ability to sense opportunities, seize them, and transform processes through reconfigurable digital tools

The chapters in this playbook illustrate three broad pathways SMEs can take:

i.   **Operations-first** — beginning with streamlining internal processes through automation, analytics, and visibility.
ii. **Market-first** — addressing external fragmentation by orchestrating customer journeys, vendor networks, and ecosystems.
iii. **Customer-first** — reengineering relationships with clients through unified CRMs, loyalty systems, and predictive engagement.

Though starting points differ, all cases converge on one insight: integration precedes innovation. Only once data and processes are connected can SMEs unlock the potential of AI, automation, and sustainability measurement.

3. Pathways Through Student Chapters

3.1. Chapter 1: Empowering Sustainable Growth with Smart IS – A Fashion SME Experience

The first student case, authored by Shaikh et al. (2025), examines sustainability-focused apparel SMEs constrained by their reliance on spreadsheets to manage sales, inventory, marketing, and sustainability reporting. This manual approach creates inefficiencies across decision-making, forecasting, and customer engagement, while also making it difficult to communicate a company's eco-friendly value proposition to stakeholders.

The proposed solution was a phased IS strategy built on the Microsoft ecosystem. Real-time dashboards through Power BI would replace manual reports, while Azure Machine Learning enabled predictive demand forecasting would optimize inventory planning. AI-enhanced segmentation would allow for more personalized marketing, while automated sustainability dashboards quantified impact metrics such as waste reduction and recycling rates. An optional chatbot proposed would further extend customer engagement, reducing response times and capturing feedback for continuous improvement.

This chapter sets the tone for the playbook by highlighting a crucial lesson: digital transformation in SMEs must begin by replacing inefficiencies at the core of operations. Without reliable data integration and automated reporting, sustainability remains rhetorical rather than measurable. By grounding transformation in everyday processes, the chapter demonstrates how technology can serve as both a competitive advantage and a vehicle for responsible growth.

3.2. Chapter 2: Intelligent & Sustainable Supply Chain for Smart Retail

Moving beyond internal operations, Tauro et al., (2025) tackle the supply chain dimension with *Intelligent & Sustainable Supply Chain for Smart Retail*, a proposal for sustainable fashion SMEs. While businesses may have functioning e-commerce platforms, often their supply chain are still monitored manually, with limited visibility across production, logistics, and delivery. This creates inefficiencies in forecasting, customer communication, and sustainability reporting.

The team's solution introduced IoT-enabled inventory management, AI-powered demand forecasting, and a sustainability tracker integrated into

17

Power BI dashboards. Customers would receive automated WhatsApp updates, while internal teams would gain visibility into waste saved and carbon reduced through real-time reporting. APIs would connect Shopify, logistics systems, and communication tools to create an intelligent, responsive, and sustainable supply chain.

The contribution of this chapter lies in its extension of operational integration to the ecosystem level. By connecting suppliers, customers, and sustainability metrics into a single flow, the case illustrates how SMEs can align efficiency, and environmental accountability. It underscores the importance of data-driven supply chains not just for resilience but also for building consumer trust in socially responsible sectors.

3.3. Chapter 3: Building a Conscious Commerce Engine: A Smart IS Framework for a UAE-based eco-friendly fashion marketplace

The third case, presented by Hussain et al. (2025), shifts focus to the market-facing side of digital transformation. Their study of UAE-based eco-fashion marketplace reveals a paradox: the platforms attract hundreds of monthly visitors but suffer from persistently low conversions, vendor management bottlenecks, and a lack of transparency in sustainability metrics.

Their proposed solution was an "integration-first" e-commerce engine that would be built on four interconnected systems: a Vendor Intelligence Engine to streamline onboarding and communication, a Customer Journey Engine to map touchpoints and personalize engagement, a Sustainability Engine to provide real-time impact tracking, and an Intelligence Engine to align forecasting, trend analysis, and pricing decisions. Together, these engines can transform such a platform from a fragmented marketplace into a data-driven enterprise.

This chapter highlights the strategic importance of turning sustainability into a customer-facing narrative. By embedding impact metrics into the shopping experience, the marketplace not only differentiated itself from competitors but also empowered consumers to make environmentally conscious choices. The lesson extends beyond eco-fashion: in markets where trust and transparency drive loyalty, SMEs must find ways to make their values visible, measurable, and actionable.

3.4. Chapter 4: Next-Gen CRMs for SMEs Next-Gen CRMs for SMEs: Enhancing Customer Engagement with RAP Plugins

Noronha et al. (2025) focus on customer engagement, one of the most pressing challenges for SMEs in the UAE. Scattered data across spreadsheets, inboxes, and chat threads leave SMEs without a single source of truth, resulting in sluggish responses and missed opportunities. Customers, accustomed to WhatsApp-based interactions and instant replies, often defect to competitors when delays occur.

The proposed solution was a modular strategy using Reusable Automation and Processing (RAP) plugins layered on top of a cloud CRM. These plugins integrated WhatsApp, Instagram, email, and web forms, creating a unified customer timeline. Automation engines would enforce response-time SLAs, send digital contracts, and flag negative sentiment for priority handling. AI services would add predictive lead scoring and sentiment detection, while dashboards offer managers real-time visibility into response times, conversions, and churn risks.

This chapter demonstrates the customer-first pathway, showing how SMEs can adopt enterprise-grade CRM capabilities at fraction of the cost through modular, scalable integrations. In a UAE market where most consumers expect responses within minutes, SMEs cannot afford disjointed engagement strategies. The RAP model provides a replicable blueprint for SMEs to achieve agility and customer intimacy without overwhelming their teams.

3.5. Chapter 5: Enabling Business Intelligence through Unified CRM Ecosystems

Building on the CRM conversation, Ranjbar et al. (2025) propose a more advanced model of CRM maturity: the Unified CRM Ecosystem. Here, the challenges identified are not just slow responses but deeply fragmented customer data, underperforming loyalty programs, and the absence of real-time insights.

Their proposed solution integrated HubSpot, WhatsApp Business API, Klaviyo, Smile.io loyalty systems, and Microsoft Power BI into a cohesive ecosystem. Customer interactions across e-commerce, email, WhatsApp, and loyalty programs would flow into a central database, enabling behavior-driven automation and real-time dashboards. Gamified rewards would encourage repeat purchases, while Power BI would provide leaders with actionable insights into retention, segmentation, and lifetime value.

The chapter highlights the evolution from fragmented fixes to holistic ecosystems. By moving beyond single integrations to fully-integrated platforms, SMEs can generate predictive intelligence, improve loyalty, and scale sustainably. In doing so, the authors show that CRM transformation is not a one-time project but an ongoing capability-building journey.

4. Synthesis: Opportunities and Challenges in the UAE SME Ecosystem

The playbook culminates with Khallouk (2025)'s comprehensive synthesis, which situates the student cases within the broader UAE entrepreneurial ecosystem. His analysis emphasizes how national strategies, and corporate initiatives create an enabling environment for SMEs, but also how everyday realities of fragmentation, blind spots, and execution gaps persist.

Drawing on the five chapters, Khallouk (2025) identifies recurring entrepreneurial pain points and shows how smart IS can transform them into pathways for value creation. He distinguishes between operations-first, platform-first, and customer-first strategies, aligning them with Vision 2031's emphasis on diversification and digitalization. Importantly, he reinforces three cross-cutting lessons: integrate before innovating, build dynamic capabilities rather than single tools, and make sustainability quantifiable and communicable.

This synthesis bridges the micro-level experiences of SMEs with the macro-level ambitions of the UAE. It demonstrates that while technology adoption is uneven, the principles of integration, automation, and sustainability can serve as guiding pillars for SMEs navigating growth in a fast-changing economy.

5. Cross-Cutting Lessons

Several themes emerge consistently across the six chapters as illustrated in Figure 1.

This Figure 1 illustrates the four key priorities shaping SME digital transformation: integration, dynamic capabilities, measurable sustainability, and ecosystem partnerships. The flow shows how unifying processes leads to agility, trust through accountability, and growth accelerated by collaboration.

6. Conclusion: Future-Proofing SMEs in the UAE

The chapters in this playbook collectively show that the future of SMEs in the UAE lies in the intelligent integration of smart IS. From fashion to supply chains, from eco-fashion marketplaces to unified CRMs, each case illustrates how technology can transform fragmentation into opportunity, and ambition into execution.

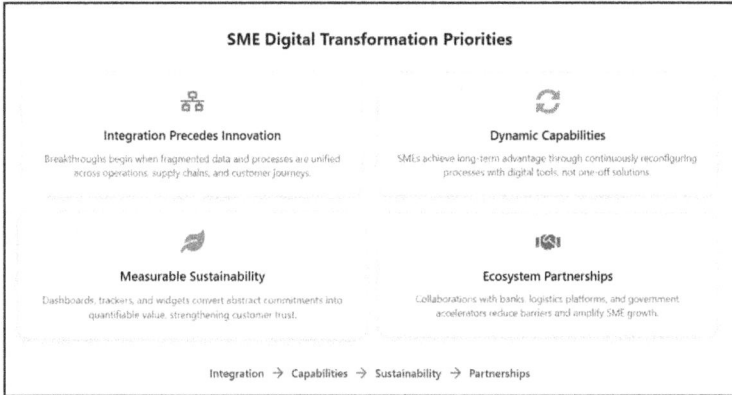

SME Digital Transformation Priorities

Integration Precedes Innovation
Breakthroughs begin when fragmented data and processes are unified across operations, supply chains, and customer journeys.

Dynamic Capabilities
SMEs achieve long-term advantage through continuously reconfiguring processes with digital tools, not one-off solutions.

Measurable Sustainability
Dashboards, trackers, and widgets convert abstract commitments into quantifiable value, strengthening customer trust.

Ecosystem Partnerships
Collaborations with banks, logistics platforms, and government accelerators reduce barriers and amplify SME growth.

Integration → Capabilities → Sustainability → Partnerships

Figure 1: SME Digital Transformation Priorities (Source: author generated)

It is also important to acknowledge that this playbook is a student-driven achievement. Each chapter represents the outcome of applied projects developed in UOWD's Information Systems courses, where students partnered with or studied SMEs in the UAE. By blending theory, practice, and creativity, through work-integrated learning, these chapters serve not only as recommendations for SMEs but also as evidence of how experiential learning can generate valuable insights for the wider business ecosystem.

As the UAE advances toward its 2031 vision, SMEs must see digital transformation not as a luxury but as a necessity. The pathway will not be identical for all: some will begin with operations, others with customer engagement, and still others with sustainability. But regardless of starting point, the destination is shared - a future where SMEs are digitally enabled, environmentally responsible, and globally competitive.

This playbook offers more than isolated cases. It provides a roadmap, grounded in real challenges and tested solutions, for how SMEs can future-proof themselves in an era of volatility and opportunity. By integrating entrepreneurship, technology, and sustainability, SMEs can not only survive but thrive as the engines of the UAE's next economic chapter.

7. References

Gulf Today. (2025, July 2). *UAE consumers lead world in mobile shopping: Visa.* Gulf Today. https://www.gulftoday.ae/news/2025/07/02/uae-consumers-lead-world-in-mobile-shopping-visa

Harmon, R, (2025, January 19). *UAE logistics providers expand same-day and next-day delivery services.* Logistics Middle East. https://www.logisticsmiddleeast.com/logistics/how-uae-logistics-providers-are-navigating-growth-and-green-goals

Hussain, T. S., Kumar, A. A., & Elgamil, M. (2025). Building a Conscious Commerce Engine: A Smart IS Framework for a UAE-based eco-friendly fashion marketplace. In Z. R. Khan, P. Bhagwat, P. Mukala, & N. Ruxwana (Eds.), *Technology adoption playbook for sustainability-focused startups and SMEs* (pp. 61-77). ENAI WG Centre for Academic Integrity in the UAE; University of Wollongong in Dubai; Gulf Book Services LTD, UK.

IFZA. (2023). *SMEs in the UAE: A comprehensive guide.* IFZA Free Zone Authority. https://ifza.com/wp-content/uploads/2023/06/Guide-7-SMEs-in-the-UAE-4.pdf

Khallouk, M (2025). Connecting the Dots: Innovation, Entrepreneurship, and the Sustainable Future. In Z. R. Khan, P. Bhagwat, P. Mukala, & N. Ruxwana (Eds.), *Technology adoption playbook for sustainability-focused startups and SMEs* (pp. 111-122). ENAI WG Centre for Academic Integrity in the UAE; University of Wollongong in Dubai; Gulf Book Services LTD, UK

Liamzon, E. (2024 October 8). *Amazon UAE and 7X join forces to accelerate sustainable last-mile delivery.* Economy Middle East. https://economymiddleeast.com/news/amazon-uae-and-7x-join-forces-to-accelerate-sustainable-last-mile-delivery

Nexdigm. (2025). *UAE logistics and warehousing market report.* Nexdigm. https://www.nexdigm.com/market-research/report-store/uae-logistics-and-warehousing-market-report/

Noronha, N., Dypiangco, R.., D'souza, F., & Mathew, N (2025). Next-Gen CRMs for SMEs: Enhancing Customer Engagement with RAP Plugins. In Z. R. Khan, P. Bhagwat, P. Mukala, & N. Ruxwana (Eds.), *Technology adoption playbook for sustainability-focused startups and SMEs* (pp. 81-95). ENAI WG Centre for Academic Integrity in the UAE; University of Wollongong in Dubai; Gulf Book Services LTD, UK.

Pearl Digital. (2025). *Why UAE businesses must embrace a mobile-first approach.* Pearl Digital. https://pearldigital.ae/why-uae-businesses-must-embrace-a-mobile-first-approach/

Ranjbar, S., Islam, F., & Virani, H. (2025). Enabling Business Intelligence through Unified CRM Ecosystems. In Z. R. Khan, P. Bhagwat, P.

Mukala, & N. Ruxwana (Eds.), *Technology adoption playbook for sustainability-focused startups and SMEs* (pp. 97-108). ENAI WG Centre for Academic Integrity in the UAE; University of Wollongong in Dubai; Gulf Book Services LTD, UK.

Shaikh, A. N., Sujith, A., Bikram, R. S., & Roy, A. (2025). Empowering Sustainable Growth with Smart IS – The Fashion SME. In Z. R. Khan, P. Bhagwat, P. Mukala, & N. Ruxwana (Eds.), *Technology adoption playbook for sustainability-focused startups and SMEs* (pp. 27–40). ENAI WG Centre for Academic Integrity in the UAE; University of Wollongong in Dubai; Gulf Book Services LTD, UK.

Shrivastava, V. K., & Riaz, S. (2023). Adoption of Big Data and AI in UAE SMEs in Unpredictable Environment. 9th 2023 International Conference on Control, Decision and Information Technologies, CoDIT 2023, 816–821 2023.

Steidle, C., Ostojic, S., Achterfeldt, S. *et al.* (2025) Small players, big impact? Unveiling practices and challenges of sustainability reporting by German SMEs. *Discov Sustain* **6**, 780 (2025). https://doi.org/10.1007/s43621-025-01727-3

Tauro, A. N., Varughese, A., Sapavat, A. S. & Arar, L. (2025). Intelligent & Sustainable Supply Chain for Smart Retail. In Z. R. Khan, P. Bhagwat, P. Mukala, & N. Ruxwana (Eds.), *Technology adoption playbook for sustainability-focused startups and SMEs* (pp. 43-58). ENAI WG Centre for Academic Integrity in the UAE; University of Wollongong in Dubai; Gulf Book Services LTD, UK.

UAE Government Portal. (2022). *Digital Economy Strategy: Dubai/UAE aims to double the contribution of the digital economy to GDP from 9.7% to 19.4% in 10 years.* Retrieved from https://u.ae/en/about-the-uae/strategies-initiatives-and-awards/strategies-plans-and-visions/finance-and-economy/digital-economy-strategy

UAE Government Portal. (2024). *"We the UAE 2031" Vision – Key National Indicators.* Official Portal of the UAE Government. Retrieved from https://u.ae/en/about-the-uae/strategies-initiatives-and-awards/strategies-plans-and-visions/innovation-and-future-shaping/we-the-uae-2031-vision

World Union of Arab Bankers [WUAB]. (2023). *SMEs in UAE.* WUAB Magazine. https://wuab.org/magazine-articles/smes-in-uae/

SECTION I
OPERATIONS-FIRST APPROACH

Chapter 1

Empowering Sustainable Growth with Smart IS: A Fashion SME Experience

Asraa Noohu Shaikh . Advaith Sujith . Rhythm Shahi Bikram . Anushka Roy

Abstract

Many sustainability-driven SMEs that manufacture and sell directly to consumers struggle with fragmented data, manual workflows, and opaque sustainability reporting. This chapter presents a practical playbook for adopting Smart Information Systems to integrate data, automate routine work, and apply light AI for daily decision-making. The modular approach uses cloud services to deliver real-time dashboards, demand forecasting, customer segmentation, and automated impact tracking, improving accuracy, speed, and transparency. The chapter outlines a phased roadmap, risks and mitigations, and concise evaluation criteria that SMEs can adapt to their scale and context. Results expected include fewer stockouts and overstocks, faster reporting, higher repeat purchases, and clearer evidence of waste and emissions reduction. By embedding sustainability indicators into core operations rather than treating them as afterthoughts, SMEs can strengthen trust, reduce costs, and grow responsibly. The framework is technology-agnostic, replicable, and suitable for any DTC SME in sustainable fashion or allied products across market contexts.

Keywords

Smart Information Systems, Sustainable SMEs, Direct-to-Consumer, Digital Transformation, Sustainability Metrics

Asraa Noohu Shaikh ✉
University of Wollongong in Dubai
abmns250@uowmail.edu.au

Advaith Sujith
University of Wollongong

Rhythm Shahi Bikram
University of Wollongong in Dubai

Anushka Roy
University of Wollongong in Dubai

Shaikh, A. N., Sujith, A., Bikram, R. S., & Roy, A. (2025). Empowering Sustainable Growth with Smart IS – The Fashion SME. In Z. R. Khan, P. Bhagwat, P. Mukala, & N. Ruxwana (Eds.), *Technology adoption playbook for sustainability-focused startups and SMEs* (pp. 27–40). ENAI WG Centre for Academic Integrity in the UAE; University of Wollongong in Dubai; Gulf Book Services LTD, UK.

1. Introduction

In today's competitive business environment, small and medium-sized enterprises (SMEs) in the fashion and retail sector are under mounting pressure to balance profitability with sustainability. Consumers in the UAE and beyond are increasingly demanding eco-friendly products, transparent supply chains, and responsive customer service, while expecting the same seamless digital experiences delivered by larger global brands. For sustainability-driven businesses, this creates a unique challenge: how to scale responsibly while maintaining the ethical values that define their brand identity. The ability to integrate sustainable practices with efficient operations has become not only a differentiator, but also a survival strategy (White et al., 2019).

Despite their agility and mission-driven focus, many SMEs struggle with fragmented systems and manual processes that limit visibility and slow decision-making. Inventory often swings between overstock and shortages, customer insights remain buried in spreadsheets, and sustainability metrics are difficult to quantify. Without data integration and automation, these enterprises risk undermining both growth and credibility in markets where consumer trust is tightly linked to transparency (Geissdoerfer et al., 2017). Against this backdrop, smart information systems (IS) offer a way forward, enabling SMEs to leverage cloud technologies, business intelligence, and light AI solutions to build operations that are not only efficient, but also aligned with sustainable growth (Laudon & Laudon, 2018).

This chapter explores the digital transformation of a UAE-based sustainable fashion SME through the lens of smart IS adoption. By examining the practical challenges of hybrid retail, the opportunities of modular cloud-based solutions, and the measurable impact of automation and analytics, it highlights how mission-driven enterprises can achieve both operational excellence and sustainability goals. The discussion also situates these insights within the wider context of SMEs in emerging markets, offering a framework that others can adapt as they navigate the twin demands of growth and responsibility (Holzinger et al., 2025; McKinsey & Company, 2017).

2. Industry Context

This chapter examines the challenges and opportunities faced by sustainability-driven SMEs that manufacture and sell ready-made garments and related products directly to consumers. The discussion draws from common pain points observed across the sector and aims to provide lessons applicable to a broad range of enterprises pursuing sustainable growth.

Business Type: Retail – Sustainability-Driven Product Manufacturing and DTC Sales

The sustainable consumer goods sector is expanding globally, with enterprises prioritizing eco-friendly production, health and safety standards, and responsible business practices. Many SMEs in this space adopt direct-to-consumer (DTC) e-commerce as their core channel, complemented by selective physical outlets or distribution partners. This model allows closer customer engagement and stronger brand identity, but also brings challenges in balancing operational efficiency, scalability, and sustainability commitments.

For these companies, digital transformation is no longer optional but a necessity to ensure scalability and competitiveness. Manual workflows in areas such as inventory control, customer data management, and sustainability reporting limit growth, slow responsiveness, and reduce transparency. By integrating smart information systems, SMEs can streamline operations, monitor environmental impact, deliver personalized customer experiences, and maintain competitiveness while staying true to their sustainability missions.

Key areas typically impacted by digital transformation include:

- Supply Chain and Production Operations
- Customer Experience and Feedback
- Sustainability Monitoring and Reporting
- Direct-to-Consumer E-commerce and Sales

3. Business Challenge – pain points

Sustainable fashion small and medium-sized enterprises (SMEs), particularly those in ready-made garment retail, often face severe operational constraints due to their heavy reliance on manual data management practices. Many of these businesses are founded on values of affordability, eco-consciousness, and consumer well-being, with a commitment to reducing the environmental impact of fast fashion and single-use materials (White et al., 2019). Their business models frequently combine DTC e-commerce with selective physical distribution, creating both opportunities for growth and challenges in maintaining efficient, sustainable operations (Geissdoerfer et al., 2017).

In practice, these SMEs may operate basic online shops that export sales data into spreadsheets, while subsequent processes, such as inventory tracking, customer analysis, marketing evaluation, and sustainability reporting, are still managed manually. Such labor-intensive workflows slow decision-making, reduce responsiveness to changing consumer demands, and make forecasting unreliable, often leading to stock imbalances (McKinsey & Company, 2017). Marketing campaigns are difficult to optimize without real-time insights, while sustainability goals are undermined by the inability to systematically measure and communicate environmental impact (Laudon & Laudon, 2018). Without automated tracking of key metrics like waste reduction or safe production practices, these enterprises face barriers to scaling effectively while staying true to their mission of promoting health, safety, and sustainability (Rathore, 2019).

4. Proposed Solution Overview

To address business inefficiencies and support long-term, sustainable growth, this chapter proposes a phased Information System (IS) strategy that emphasizes Data Integration, Automation, and light Artificial Intelligence (AI) solutions. The proposed architecture has been designed to address both current operational pain points and future scalability goals. The key components of the proposed solution are:

- Real-time business dashboards with Power BI (Siva, 2023) to replace manual spreadsheet reports, offering a dynamic view of marketing, sales, and inventory performance.
- Simple AI-powered demand forecasting by using Azure Machine Learning's (Microsoft, 2025a) predictive capabilities that leverage historical trends and forecast demand to improve inventory planning and reduce overstock.
- Customer insights segmentation through AI-enhanced segmentation using clustering tools in Power BI (Microsoft, 2023a) to surface meaningful customer segments based on real purchase behavior, enabling more personalized and cost-effective marketing campaigns.
- Automated sustainability tracking dashboards using Power BI dataflows (Siva, 2023) that automatically measure, visualize, and quantify impact metrics, such as waste reduction from reusable products.
- An optional proposal for implementing a conversational AI chatbot using Power Virtual Agents (Microsoft, 2023b) to improve customer support, automate responses to common customer queries, and gather user feedback, which further improves the accuracy of customer insights (Harinayaranan, 2021).

The scalable and user-friendly design of this modular and adaptable system ensures that SMEs may progressively integrate new technology without overburdening their internal processes.

5. Technologies Involved

Proposed to be built on the Microsoft ecosystem, the framework combines business intelligence, AI-driven insights, and automated data processing to transform operations. The following are some of the core technologies involved in the proposed solution:

- **Data Integration**
  Azure Data Factory (ADF): Cloud-based Extract, Transform, Load (ETL) pipelines that automate data collection and transformation from various sources into ready-to-use information for analysis and reporting (Rawat & Narain, 2019).
  Power BI Dataflows: Enables reusable data transformation logic across an enterprise for the creation of new reports and dashboards (Siva, 2023).
  Power Query: Intuitive data connection and transformation tool integrated within Power BI and ADF's dataflows for cleaning and shaping raw data without extensive coding (Microsoft, 2025b).

- **Storage**
  Azure SQL Database: a fully managed, scalable relational database service that ensures high availability, robust security, and automated backups, making it ideal for modern applications with dynamic workloads, while also providing advanced query processing features for optimized performance (Microsoft, 2025a; Ward, 2024).

- **AI & Machine Learning**
  Power BI AI Clustering: Automated customer segmentation to provide in-depth analysis (Microsoft, 2023a).
  Q/A visuals: Natural Language Processing (NLP) interface that transforms business questions into visualizations for intuitive data exploration (Microsoft, 2025a).

- **Optional Add-ons**
  Azure Machine Learning: Helps in optimizing stock levels and predicting trends using demand forecasting and predictive models (Microsoft, 2025a).
  Power Virtual Agents: AI-powered chatbots that require no code to handle FAQs (Microsoft, 2023b).

5.1. Proposed Solution Architecture

The proposed solution is designed in a simplified manner to align with technical capabilities and provide a financially viable option that is user-friendly, scalable, and capable of addressing urgent business needs, as illustrated in the high-level solution architecture view in Figure 1.

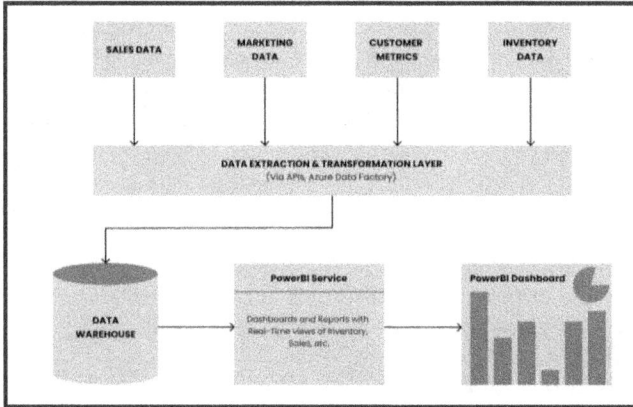

Figure 1: Solution workflow (Source: developed by authors as a sample)

Figure 1 displays a simple workflow of the application. It starts with data from numerous sources, such as Sales, Marketing, Customer, and Inventory data, being retrieved and converted using APIs and ETL tools like Power Query and Azure Data Factory. The processed data is then subsequently saved in a data warehouse, which would be created using Azure SQL Database. The Power BI Service sits on top of this layer, generating real-time dashboards and reports that combine data on sales trends, customer behaviour, marketing trends, sustainability score, and more. Users may access these insights via a user-friendly Power BI dashboard, which can be accessed via web or mobile.

6. Data Use & Analytics

To enable robust, data-driven decision-making, the proposed solution leverages a broad range of structured and semi-structured data streams. These data streams include transactional records (e.g.: orders, payments, refunds), marketing metrics (e.g.: email campaign open rates, social media ad interactions), behavioral indicators (e.g.: web page views, click-through rates, time-on-sites), and customer demographic profiles (e.g.: age, location, repeat purchase behavior).

With the use of automated ETL pipelines, all collected data is systematically

33

extracted. The ETL pipelines are designed to normalize and clean data from various sources, including e-commerce platforms, CRM systems, and marketing tools (Rawat & Narain, 2019; AWS, 2025). Eventually, the information is then stored securely in a cloud-based data warehouse that facilitates multi-source integration and scalability (AWS, 2025).

Business Intelligence (BI) pulls data from this warehouse to enable real-time interactive dashboards that visualize Key Performance Indicators (KPIs) such as customer churn rates, daily revenues, and sustainability scores. Through these dashboards, decision-makers can respond quickly to changes in the market and client demands (Hashemi-Pour & Sutner, 2024; Yerra, 2025).

Furthermore, Artificial Intelligence (AI) models such as unsupervised clustering algorithms and time-series forecasts are deployed to detect hidden patterns and trends. Forecasting technologies help to synchronize production and reduce waste by predicting future product demand and seasonal variations (Makridakis et al., 2018). Additionally, customer segmentation helps to personalize marketing strategies and product recommendations by identifying valuable consumer groups based on their behavior (Rodrigues et al., 2025). This research supports the benefits of time-series forecasting and clustering methods in retail analysis. Time-series forecasting is frequently used to enhance inventory control and demand prediction (Makridakis et al., 2018). However, it has been established that clustering methods, such as K-means, improve the precision of client segmentation and marketing personalization (Rodrigues et al. 2025).

Figure 2 is a prototype dashboard illustrating how data from various sources, such as e-commerce, marketing, customer activity, etc., can be unified or integrated into an interactive Power BI interface:

Figure 2: Figma Prototype of Dashboard (Source: developed by authors as a sample)

By ensuring operations are not just data-informed but also proactive and flexible, this strategic use of analytics enables the business to improve profitability and sustainability while continuously improving its services and reducing operational barriers.

7. Benefits

The proposed Smart IS solution transforms SME's operations by replacing fragmented, manual processes with an integrated, data-driven framework that delivers measurable improvements across their key areas:

- **Streamlined Operations:** Automated reporting with Power BI dashboards saves hours of manual work each week. Real-time data access helps decision-makers respond quickly to inventory, sales, and supplier trends, improving agility and reducing delays (Yerra, 2025).
- **Inventory Optimization:** AI-driven demand forecasting reduces prediction errors by 20–50%, improving accuracy in inventory planning and demand management (McKinsey & Company, 2017).
- **Customer Engagement:** Customer segmentation based on purchase behavior and demographics enables targeted marketing, replacing ineffective generic campaigns and fostering long-term loyalty (Wavetec, 2024).
- **Sustainability Impact:** Automated tracking of metrics such as recycling rates and waste reduction provides verifiable sustainability evidence, reduces overproduction, and identifies opportunities for improvement (Rathore, 2019).
- **Future-Ready Foundation:** The scalable system grows with SME needs, supports new technologies, and ensures continuity while adapting to evolving markets and sustainability standards.

8. Risk and Considerations

Although the proposed Smart IS solution offers numerous benefits, several potential risks and limitations must be addressed for it to be implemented successfully. These considerations reflect well-established risks in digital transformation and IS adoption projects (Laudon & Laudon, 2018). These considerations must be factored into budgeting, planning, and management:

- Without structured training, non-technical users may struggle to adopt BI and AI tools, limiting ROI (Crudu, 2024).
- Siloed systems, inconsistent formats, or incomplete records can

undermine accuracy, making data cleansing essential.

- Cloud solutions require secure connectivity and strong cybersecurity, including encryption, multifactor authentication (MFA), and role-based controls
- Analytics should support, not replace, human oversight; over-reliance risks poor decisions (Holzinger et al., 2025).
- Ongoing expenses for storage, subscriptions, and upgrades must be budgeted, while vendor lock-in poses added risks.
- Employees may resist new workflows; effective change management and communication are critical.

9. Evaluation Criteria

To assess the success of the proposed digital transformation, a set of Key Performance Indicators (KPIs) is defined across core business areas. These indicators measure operational efficiency, customer engagement, sustainability, and overall impact. Targets are aligned with industry best practices while reflecting realistic improvements for SMEs.

Table 1: Proposed Evaluation Criteria and Key Performance Indicators (KPIs) (Source: developed by authors as sample)

Area	KPI	Target
Inventory Management	Stockout rate, Overstock frequency	<5% stockouts, <10% overstock
Demand Forecasting	Forecast accuracy vs. actual sales	≥85% accuracy
Customer Engagement	Repeat purchase rate, NPS (Net Promoter Score)	>30% repeat purchases, NPS > 50
Operational Efficiency	Order fulfilment time, Reporting hours saved	20% faster fulfilment, <2 hrs weekly
Sustainability	Textile waste reduction, Emission tracking	Visible year-on-year improvement

10. Sustainability Alignment

The proposed digital solution is mainly designed to strengthen and complement the SME's sustainability mission. This solution demonstrates how technology and sustainability may coexist peacefully, improving both environmental responsibility and operational efficiency rather than being viewed as conflicting concerns.

- Improved inventory turnover and AI-based demand forecasting reduce overproduction, obsolescence, and textile waste, aligning with circular economy principles (Geissdoerfer et al., 2017).
- Live dashboards track packaging, emissions, and transport efficiency, enabling stakeholders to verify environmental performance.
- Cloud-optimized services and lightweight AI models minimize energy use. Providers such as Microsoft Azure are committed to renewable energy and carbon-negative operations (Microsoft, 2025a; Ruiz, 2024).
- AI-driven customer segmentation reduces irrelevant advertising, ensuring targeted campaigns that align with ethical standards and reduce digital waste.

11. Conclusion

Sustainability-driven SMEs in ready-made fashion and related consumer sectors operate at the intersection of growth and responsibility. As this chapter has outlined, dependence on manual workflows creates inefficiencies that restrict competitiveness and weaken the credibility of sustainability claims. Smart Information Systems (IS) provide a pathway forward by enabling integration, automation, and data-driven decision-making. Through dashboards, predictive analytics, and customer segmentation, SMEs can reduce waste, optimize inventory, enhance engagement, and demonstrate measurable sustainability impact. These outcomes not only improve operational efficiency but also align with consumer expectations for transparency and ethical production.

The broader lesson is that digital transformation, when designed with sustainability in mind, can serve as a catalyst rather than a compromise. A phased, modular approach allows SMEs to scale responsibly, balancing immediate needs with long-term adaptability. By embedding sustainability indicators into core systems and leveraging technologies such as cloud services and AI-driven insights, SMEs can strengthen stakeholder trust, respond quickly to changing market demands, and future-proof their operations. In a landscape where environmental and social accountability are becoming non-negotiable, the integration of smart IS is not simply a technical upgrade but a strategic imperative for sustainable growth.

12. Acknowledgement

This chapter utilizes generative AI to assist with language refinement and grammatical improvements. However, all ideas, core concepts, structures, and frameworks were entirely developed by the authors.

13. References

AWS (2025). *What is data analytics?*. Amazon Web Services. Available at: https://aws.amazon.com/what-is/data-analytics/

Crudu, A. (2024, March). The Importance of User Training in Enterprise Software Adoption. MoldStud. https://moldstud.com/articles/p-the-importance-of-user-training-in-enterprise-software-adoption

Geissdoerfer, M., Savaget, P., Bocken, N.M. & Hultink, E.J., (2017). The Circular Economy—A new sustainability paradigm?. *Journal of cleaner production, 143*, pp.757-768. https://www.sciencedirect.com/science/article/abs/pii/S0959652616321023

Hashemi-Pour, C., & Sutner, S. (2024, October). *Business intelligence dashboard.* TechTarget. https://www.techtarget.com/searchbusinessanalytics/definition/business-intelligence-dashboard

Holzinger, A., Zatloukal, K., & Muller, H. (2025). Is human oversight to AI systems still possible? *New Biotechnology, 85*, 59-62. https://doi.org/10.1016/j.nbt.2024.12.003

Laudon, JP & Laudon, KC (2018), *Management information systems : managing the digital firm*, Pearson, Harlow. (Accessed through UOW Library)

Makridakis, S., Spiliotis, E. & Assimakopoulos, V., (2018). Statistical and Machine Learning forecasting methods: Concerns and ways forward. *PLoS ONE 13(3): e0194889. https://doi.org/10.1371/journal.pone.0194889*

McKinsey & Company. (2017). Smartening up with artificial intelligence: How AI will transform Germany's industrial sector. McKinsey & Company. https://www.mckinsey.com/~/media/mckinsey/industries/semiconductors/our%20insights/smartening%20up%20with%20artificial%20intelligence/smartening-up-with-artificial-intelligence.pdf

Microsoft. (2023b). Power Virtual Agents: 2023 release wave 1. Microsoft Learn.

Microsoft. (2023b). *Explore Q&A in Power BI.* Microsoft Learn.

Microsoft. (2025a). *Azure Machine Learning.* Microsoft Azure. Available at: https://learn.microsoft.com/en-us/azure/machine-learning/overview-what-is-azure-machine-learning?view=azureml-api-2

Microsoft. (2025a). *What is Power Query?* Microsoft Learn. Available at: https://learn.microsoft.com/en-us/power-query/power-query-what-is-power-query

Harinayaranan, V. P. (2021). *Building the modern workplace with SharePoint Online: Solutions with SPFx, Power Automate, Power Apps, Teams, and PVA.* Apress. https://doi.org/10.1007/978-1-4842-6945-9

Rathore, B., (2019). Artificial intelligence in sustainable fashion marketing: Transforming the supply chain landscape. *Eduzone: International Peer Reviewed/Refereed Multidisciplinary Journal*, 8(2), 25–38. Retrieved from https://eduzonejournal.com/index.php/eiprmj/article/view/36 3

Rawat, S., & Narain, A. (2019). Introduction to Azure Data Factory. In: Understanding Azure Data Factory. Apress, Berkeley, CA. https://doi.org/10.1007/978-1-4842-4122-6 2

Rodrigues, G. N., Hossain Mir, M. D. N., Bhuiyan, M. D. S. M., *et al.*, (2025). NLP-driven customer segmentation: A comprehensive review of methods and applications in personalized marketing. *Data Science and Management.* Advance online publication. https://doi.org/10.1016/j.dsm.2025.09.002

Ruiz, L. (2024, August 8). *Sustainable development: Minimizing digital footprint and optimizing consumption.* Sngular. Available at: https://www.sngular.com/insights/340/sustainable-development-minimizing-digital-footprint-and-optimizing-consumption

Siva, B. (2023). *How and when to use dataflows in Power BI.* phData. Available at: https://www.phdata.io/blog/how-and-when-to-use-dataflows-in-power-bi/

Ward, B. (2024). What Is Azure SQL?. In: Azure SQL Revealed. Apress, Berkeley, CA. https://doi.org/10.1007/979-8-8688-0974-3 2

Wavetec (2024). *Customer segmentation: Benefits & definition.* Available at: https://www.wavetec.com/blog/customer-segmentation-benefits-definition/

White, K., Habib, R., & Hardisty, D. J. (2019). How to SHIFT Consumer Behaviors to be More Sustainable: A Literature Review and Guiding Framework. *Journal of Marketing, 83*(3), 22-49. https://doi.org/10.1177/0022242919825649 (Original work published 2019)

Yerra, S., (2025). Enhancing inventory management through real-time Power BI dashboards and KPI tracking. *Int. J. Sci. Res. Comput. Sci. Eng. Inf. Technol.* DOI: 10.32628/CSEIT25112458

Chapter 2

Intelligent & Sustainable Supply Chain for Smart Retail

Ashton Vivian Tauro . Abel Varughese . Aagna Samhita Sapavat . Loulieh
Arar

Abstract
This chapter examines how intelligent and sustainable supply chains can
strengthen the growth and resilience of retail enterprises in the UAE,
particularly in the sustainable fashion and consumer goods sectors.
Although many businesses have embraced e-commerce, their backend
operations often remain fragmented and manual, leading to inefficiencies,
weak demand forecasting, and poor sustainability tracking. To address these
challenges, the chapter introduces a digitally enabled supply chain
framework based on UAE market case. The framework proposes to
integrate emerging technologies such as IoT for real-time inventory
visibility, AI for demand forecasting and customer insights, and Power BI
for data visualization and reporting. A proposed sustainability tracker
further measures waste reduction, emissions, and resource efficiency in
alignment with the UAE Green Agenda 2030. Prototype dashboards
illustrate how these tools improve decision-making, customer satisfaction,
and transparency, enabling enterprises to enhance efficiency, build trust,
and advance national sustainability goals

Keywords
Sustainable Supply Chain, Smart Retail, Digital Transformation, Artificial
Intelligence (AI), UAE Green Agenda 2030

Ashton Vivian Tauro ✉
University of Wollongong in Dubai
avt999@uowmail.edu.au

Abel Varughese
University of Wollongong in Dubai

Aagna Samhita Sapavat
University of Wollongong in Dubai

Loulieh Arar
University of Wollongong in Dubai

41

Tauro, A. N., Varughese, A., Sapavat, A. S. & Arar, L. (2025). Intelligent & Sustainable Supply Chain for Smart Retail. In Z. R. Khan, P. Bhagwat, P. Mukala, & N. Ruxwana (Eds.), *Technology adoption playbook for sustainability-focused startups and SMEs* (pp. 43-58). ENAI WG Centre for Academic Integrity in the UAE; University of Wollongong in Dubai; Gulf Book Services LTD, UK.

1. Introduction

The rapid evolution of smart retail has placed supply chains at the forefront of innovation, demanding not only operational efficiency but also sustainability as a core value. Traditional supply chain models, often reliant on manual processes and fragmented systems, are no longer sufficient to meet the needs of eco-conscious consumers or the agility required by competitive markets. In the UAE, where sustainable retail is emerging as both a social responsibility and a strategic differentiator, digital transformation offers a pathway to resilience (UAE Government, 2024). By embedding intelligence into supply chain operations through IoT, AI, and data visualization, enterprises can achieve real-time visibility, optimize decision-making, and align with global sustainability goals.

This chapter presents a practitioner-focused digital transformation framework for SMEs in the sustainable retail sector, informed by a representative case from the UAE market. The proposed solution leverages IoT-enabled inventory management, AI-powered demand forecasting, smart customer feedback systems, and sustainability impact trackers, all visualized through intuitive dashboards. Rather than serving as a theoretical model, this framework is designed to provide actionable insights that SMEs can adapt to their own contexts. In doing so, it demonstrates how smart supply chains can act as a catalyst for growth, innovation, and sustainability in retail.

2. Industry Context

In this chapter, a sustainable fashion and ready-made garment SME in the UAE is analysed as a representative case. The proposed solution addresses common industry pain points identified through research and collaborations with businesses in the sector, with the aim of offering transferable lessons for practice.

Business Type: Retail – Sustainable Fashion Marketplace

The sustainable consumer goods sector in the UAE, particularly in health, personal care, and fashion, is increasingly adopting direct-to-consumer models, with online platforms serving as the primary channel for marketing and sales.

For companies in this sector, digital transformation is no longer optional but essential to achieve scalability and competitiveness. Traditional supply chain and retail processes are often slow, manual, and difficult to monitor, limiting growth and efficiency. By integrating digital tools, businesses can streamline operations, strengthen sustainability tracking, deliver more personalized shopping experiences, and expand their reach to wider customer segments, all while maintaining an eco-friendly focus.

Key departments typically impacted by digital transformation include:
- Supply Chain and Operations
- Customer Experience and Feedback
- Sustainability Monitoring
- E-commerce and Sales

3. Business Challenges – pain points

A sustainable fashion or ready-made garment company in the UAE faces a few interrelated operational and strategic challenges, especially when its backend operations and supply chain are largely manual, disconnected, or not systematically integrated. These challenges hinder not only efficiency, but also the ability to deliver on sustainability and brand reputation, which are becoming increasingly important in this market:

- **Limited real-time visibility into inventory and logistics**
  Sustainable fashion and garment retailers in the UAE often operate across multiple sales channels (online platforms, physical stores, and distribution hubs), which makes synchronization of stock levels and logistics data difficult without digital integration. This lack of visibility results in inaccurate inventory counts, delayed deliveries, and customer dissatisfaction. Reports on the UAE fashion retail sector highlight "supply chain complexity" as a top barrier, particularly due to fragmented import/export operations and cross-border logistics (Vinculum Group, 2024). Similar studies have shown that UAE firms adopting IoT and advanced tracking systems achieve stronger operational resilience and customer trust (Tracteck, 2025).
- **Disconnected customer feedback loops, making it difficult to improve products**
  In the UAE fashion market, personalization and rapid response to consumer preferences are critical, yet many SMEs rely on ad-hoc tools (WhatsApp, social media) that are not integrated into decision-making systems. This leads to missed insights on quality, fit, or sustainability expectations. Research indicates that UAE consumers, especially younger, urban segments, expect brands to be responsive to their feedback and willing to adapt products accordingly (Nguyen, 2025; Vinculum Group, 2024). Without systematic mechanisms to collect and act upon feedback, firms

risk alienating eco-conscious consumers who prioritize authenticity and transparency.

- **Ineffective demand forecasting, resulting in overstocking or stockouts**

  Manual forecasting methods in UAE garment businesses often fail to account for seasonality, fast fashion cycles, and regional festivals, leading to either overproduction or stockouts. Overstocking ties up working capital and increases waste, while stockouts damage customer loyalty. Research on AI in UAE supply chains has shown that predictive analytics significantly improves forecast accuracy, enabling SMEs to reduce procurement costs and inventory misalignments (Tsidulko, 2024; Saxena & Fernandes, 2025). Moreover, Abu Dhabi's Advanced Trade and Logistics Platform (ATLP) demonstrates how predictive technologies are being institutionalized in the region to prevent inefficiencies (Saxena & Fernandes, 2025).

- **Lack of sustainability tracking, which weakens the brand eco-friendly image**

  Consumers in the UAE increasingly demand transparency in how sustainable garments are sourced, manufactured, and delivered. However, without integrated sustainability trackers, SMEs cannot credibly measure or report on their environmental impact, whether in terms of carbon emissions, water use, or waste reduction. This undermines their eco-friendly positioning and exposes them to accusations of "greenwashing." Studies of the UAE fashion sector identify key barriers to sustainable retail adoption, including limited availability of green raw materials, weak regulatory frameworks, and inadequate waste management systems (Hadjielias, et al. 2021; Sarmah, 2024). These challenges emphasize the need for digital systems that make sustainability metrics visible both internally and to customers, in line with the UAE Green Agenda 2030 (UAE Government, 2024).

Without a modern, integrated system, the company risks facing reduced customer satisfaction, poor inventory control, and an inability to grow sustainably across the region.

4. Proposed Solution

The legacy systems used by such a business may include Shopify for managing the online storefront and order capture, Shiplifier for coordinating courier and logistics services, and WhatsApp for Business for direct customer communication and feedback.

We propose a new digitally enabled Operations and Supply Chain Management System integrated into the company's existing platform which includes the following features:

- IoT Enabled Real-Time Inventory Management: Smart sensors track stock levels and movement in warehouses and distribution centers. Inventory records update automatically, and alerts notify the team when restocking is needed, preventing stockouts and overstocking.
- AI Powered Demand Forecasting Engine: Analyzes historical sales, customer behaviour, marketing campaigns, and seasonal trends. AI predicts future demand, helping the company optimize purchasing and stocking decisions.
- Smart Feedback & Messaging Engine: Sends automated, personalized WhatsApp messages to customers based on orders and preferences. AI analyzes replies and survey responses to generate insights for product improvements and demand planning.
- Sustainability Impact Tracker: Calculates and visualizes environmental impact (waste saved, carbon reduced) from product sales and logistics. AI enhances projections using sales forecasts. Results are displayed in Power BI for internal use and converted into easy-to-read impact summaries for the customers, which can be found on our website or included in email receipts.
- Real-Time Inventory Sync: Connects Shopify, warehouse, and courier systems through APIs. Stock changes are immediately updated across all platforms, ensuring accurate product availability and reducing fulfilment errors.
- Power BI Dashboards: Provides actionable analytics on supply chain performance, inventory turnover, fulfilment rates, sustainability and customer satisfaction.

All system components are proposed to be safely hosted in the cloud, with a centralized database enabling real-time data exchange, AI analysis, and dashboard reporting across company's supply chain.

This integrated system is proposed to ensure that the company's supply chain becomes intelligent, responsive, and sustainability driven.

5. Technologies Involved

- IoT – Tracks inventory in real-time and the movement of products in and out of warehouses, triggering re-stock alerts when required.

- AI – Demand forecasting; feedback tagging and categorization.
- Power BI – Visualizes key supply chain metrics such as inventory turnover, stock-out frequency, lead time, order fulfilment rates, and customer feedback insights for data-driven decisions.
- Integration tools (APIs) – Seamlessly connects Shopify, Shiplifier, and WhatsApp Business to synchronize inventory, order status, and customer communication in real time.
  (Note: While APIs are not classified as emerging technologies, their evolving ecosystem plays a critical role in integrating emerging systems seamlessly.)

6. System Diagram

Figure 1 illustrates the proposed system architecture, developed by the authors using draw.io. The design integrates multiple layers to create an intelligent and sustainable supply chain. At the frontend layer, customer feedback channels and e-commerce platforms (e.g., Shopify, WhatsApp Business) capture orders and interactions. These feed into the integration layer, where APIs and IoT-enabled middleware synchronize data across logistics, warehouses, and courier systems. The backend layer centralizes data storage and analysis, enabling AI-driven demand forecasting, sustainability tracking, and performance reporting. User roles, including customers, operations teams, managers, and sustainability coordinators, interact with the system through tailored interfaces, ensuring that insights flow across all levels. Overall, the architecture demonstrates how data is collected, integrated, and transformed into actionable insights that support efficiency, customer engagement, and sustainability goals.

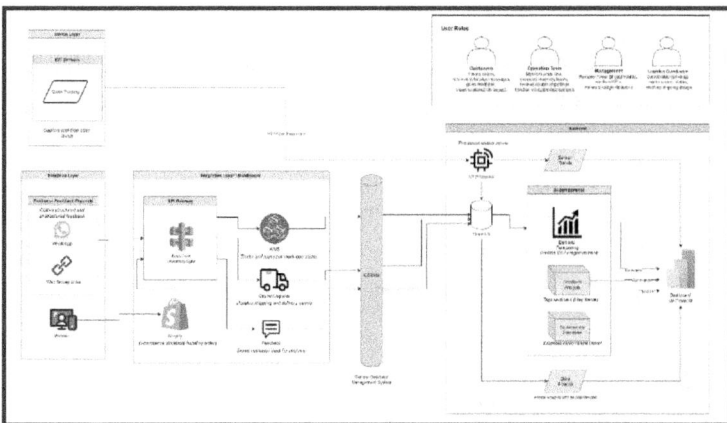

Figure 1. System Architecture (Source: developed by authors as a sample)

7. Data Use

In the proposed system, data is the backbone of building an intelligent and sustainable supply chain. This section outlines how information is systematically collected from IoT sensors, AI forecasting, customer feedback, and sustainability metrics, visualized through centralized dashboards, and applied to guide smarter decisions in procurement, logistics, customer engagement, and environmental reporting.

7.1 Data Collection

- IoT sensors track inventory movement and stock levels in real time.
- AI systems gather historical sales, seasonal demand, advertisement performance, and customer behaviour to forecast demand (Tsidulko, 2024).
- Customer feedback is collected via WhatsApp and online surveys and gets automatically tagged by AI.
- Sustainability data (waste saved, emissions reduced) are calculated using sales and logistics information.

7.2 Data Visualisation

For operational teams to monitor performance and spot bottlenecks, data is provided in a centralized, interactive format.

To demonstrate the proposed intelligent and sustainable supply chain system, prototype dashboards were developed using Power BI. These dashboards allow users to quickly interpret live business data, identify trends, and make informed decisions through clear, visually appealing displays. The prototypes integrate data from operations, logistics, customer feedback, and sustainability metrics into user-friendly formats.

- Figure 2 shows the Dashboard Page, which provides a high-level snapshot of sales performance, operations efficiency, sustainability indicators, and customer growth across different regions. This overview helps management monitor performance at a glance.
- Figure 3 illustrates the Inventory Page, which tracks bin-level stock levels, highlights low or excess stock, and uses AI to generate suggested reorder points. By combining real-time data with forecasting, the system ensures better stock control and reduces both overstocking and stockouts.
- Figure 4 presents the Logistics Page, which focuses on courier performance and order fulfilment speed. It includes comparative courier performance metrics and

regional delivery delays, enabling the company to identify bottlenecks and optimize logistics partnerships.

- Figure 5 displays the Feedback Page, which aggregates customer sentiment analysis, categorizes top feedback themes, and presents recent customer messages. This provides actionable insights into service quality and consumer expectations, closing the loop between customer experience and operations.
- Figure 6 highlights the Sustainability Tracker Page, which visualizes environmental impact by product category. Key indicators such as waste saved, CO_2 reduction, and water savings are tracked and presented in easy-to-understand graphs. This strengthens the company's eco-friendly brand positioning and supports transparent sustainability reporting.

7.3 Decision-Making Applications

- Supports decisions about procurement, logistics, inventory, and restocking in real time.
- Uses feedback analysis to inform improvements to the product and customer experience.
- Improves sustainability communication by making impact data transparent for customer interactions and internal reporting.

8. Benefits

The integration of IoT-enabled real-time inventory tracking minimizes the risks associated with overstocking and stockouts, ensuring optimal stock levels. On top of that, AI-driven demand planning boosts operational accuracy by syncing production and purchasing with the ever-changing trends in customer demand (Tsidulko, 2024).

A strong customer insight loop, made possible by automated feedback collection, not only sharpens forecasting but also plays a key role in better product development and enhancing customer experiences (Nguyen, 2022).

Sustainability reporting gets a boost through data-driven monitoring of environmental impacts, promoting transparency and improving brand reputation.

Decision-making speeds up thanks to tools like Power BI, which provide management with timely, evidence-based insights. Plus, integrated systems enhance scalability by streamlining operations, making the supply chain more agile and responsive.

All in all, operational efficiency sees a significant lift by cutting down on manual tasks and optimizing order fulfillment processes for quicker and more accurate results.

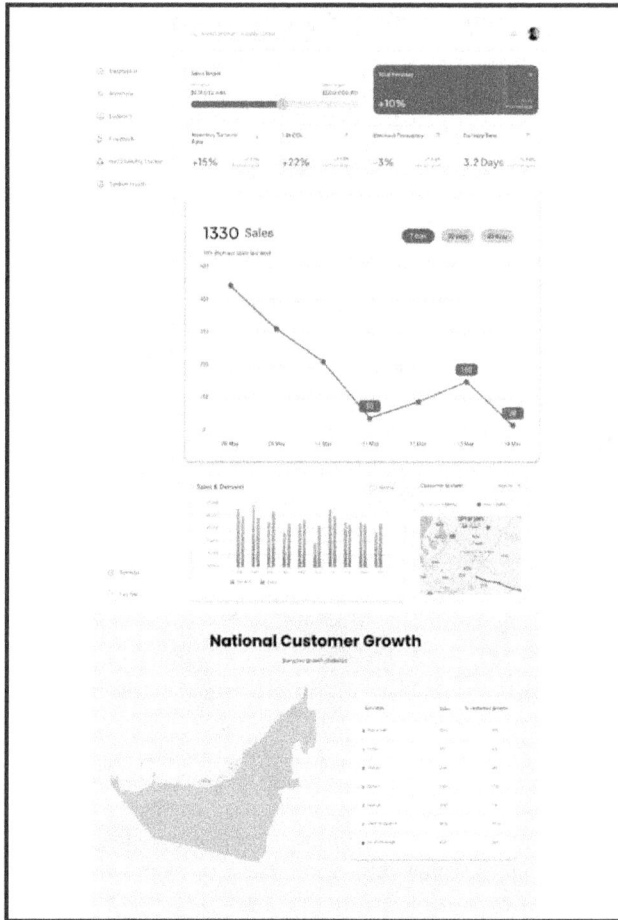

Figure 2. Dashboard Page – Provides a snapshot of sales, operations, sustainability metrics, and customer growth across regions. (Source: developed by authors as a sample)

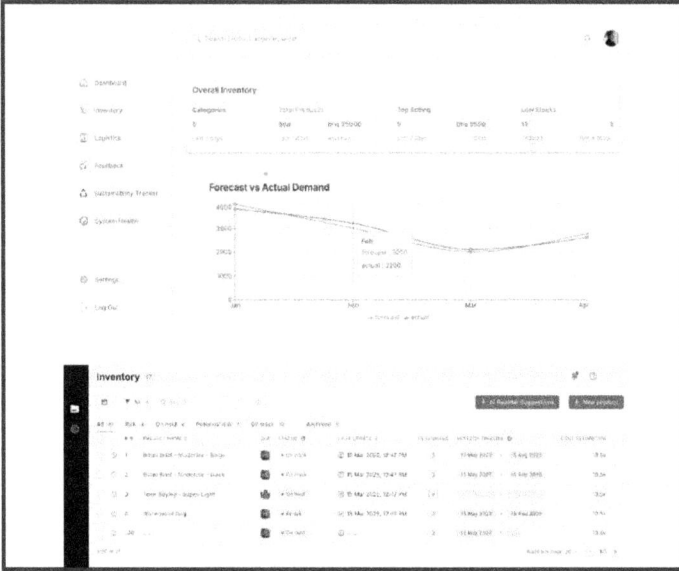

Figure 3. Inventory Page – Tracks bin-level stock, identifies low/high stock, and AI-suggested reorders. (Source: developed by authors as a sample)

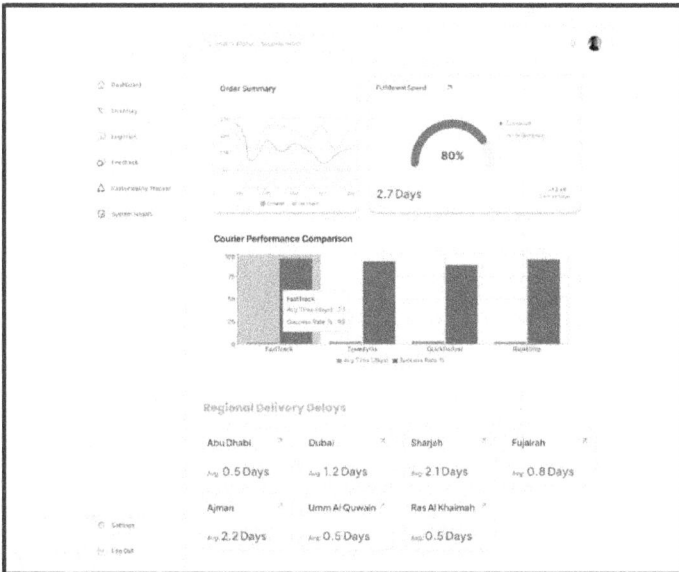

Figure 4. Logistics Page – Shows courier performance, fulfilment speed, and regional delivery delays. (Source: developed by authors as a sample)

51

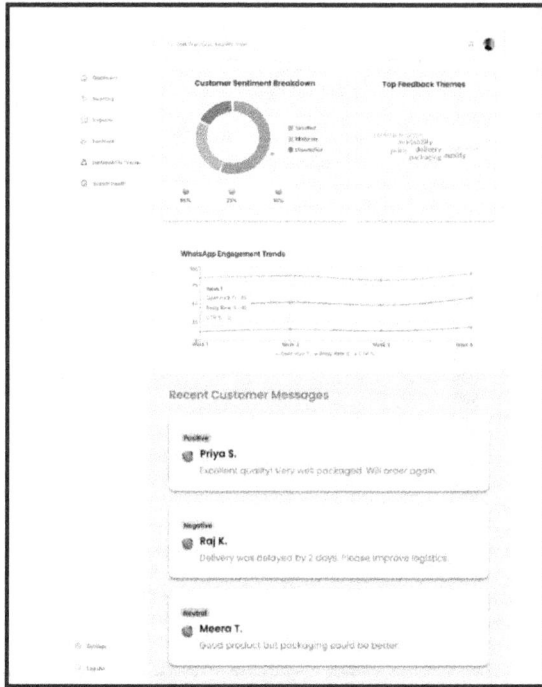

Figure 5. Feedback Page – Provides customer sentiment analysis, top themes, and recent customer messages (Source: developed by authors as a sample)

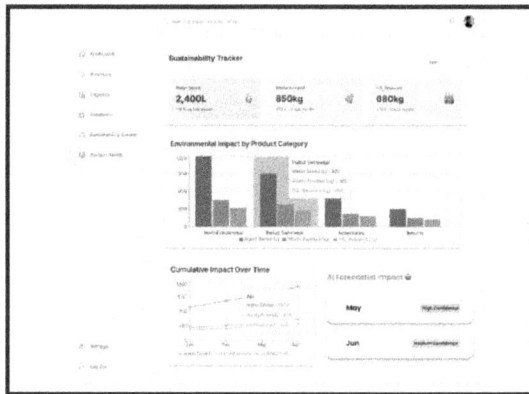

Figure 6 Sustainability Tracker Page – Displays waste saved, CO$_2$ reduction, and environmental impact by product category Source: developed by authors as a sample

9. Risks & Considerations

- Data Privacy & Security: The use of real-time tracking, AI analytics, and automated customer feedback systems increases the volume of sensitive data captured. If the integration does not have sufficient encryption or control mechanisms, as well as regional law compliance, the firm faces the risk of privacy and reputational damages (Gomstyn & Jonker, 2024).

- System Integration Challenges: Successful implementation of the digital solution relies on the ability of different systems to communicate via API. Poor integration of the mentioned systems may lead to stale data for inventory, hampering inventory synchronization, order processing, customer engagement workflows and operations continuity.

- Workforce Readiness: The shift from a manual to an automated and data-centered approach comes with a need for reskilling of personnel. Unwillingness to adopt new ways of working or a lack of tool knowledge can slow down adoption. Comprehensive onboarding, ongoing training, proactive change management, and defined restructuring plans will be necessary.

- Limits of Predictive AI: Forecasting tools based on AI technology rely on historical and behavioral information. This information may not capture unprecedented events or fast fluctuations in the market. Automation reliance with no manual checking may cause strategic misalignment, poor decisions, or inventory misalignment.

- Cost of Adoption: IoT implementation, AI analytics, and cloud infrastructure adoption comes with costs that could be detrimental to the financial structure of the company. Ailing SMEs must consider budget limits alongside return on investments.

- Downtime & Reliability Risks: As more businesses adopt third-party systems, the number of businesses reliant on digital systems simultaneously increases, which increases the chances of outsourcers halting service, outages, or technical glitches. These elements make it very hard to guarantee reliability, thus requiring separate agreements that elaborate on redundancy planning, backup protocols, and SLAs.

10. Evaluation Criteria

Authors propose these evaluation criteria (See Table 1) and KPI targets based on what we believe the proposed system needs to achieve for the company to succeed in operations, customer experience, and sustainability. While the targets follow general industry best practices (Slack, Brandon-Jones, & Burgess, 2022; Reichheld, 2003; Seuring & Müller, 2008), the specific numbers reflect our own goals and expectations.

Table 1. Proposed Evaluation Criteria and Key Performance Indicators (Source: developed by authors as sample)

Area	KPI	Target
Inventory Management	Stockout rate, Overstock frequency	<5% stockouts, <10% overstock
Demand Forecasting	Forecast accuracy vs actual sales	≥85% accuracy
Customer Experience	Feedback response rate, NPS (Net Promoter Score)	≥75% response rate, NPS > 50
Operational Efficiency	Order fulfilment time, Manual task reduction	20% faster fulfilment
Sustainability	Waste saved, Carbon offset, Customer impact awareness	Visible YoY improvement

11. Sustainability Alignment

If implemented, this solution has the potential to support sustainability by enabling SMEs to

- Reduce overproduction and avoid unnecessary waste.
- Promote long-lasting, reusable products over disposables.
- Clearly measure and share environmental savings with customers.
- Supports UN Sustainable Development Goal 12: Responsible Consumption.

12. Conclusion

The transformation of supply chains into intelligent and sustainable systems is no longer a strategic choice but a necessity for retail enterprises in the UAE, especially within the sustainable fashion and consumer goods sectors. As highlighted throughout this chapter, the reliance on manual and fragmented operations creates inefficiencies, limits visibility, and weakens sustainability commitments, factors that can undermine both growth and brand reputation in a rapidly evolving market. By adopting advanced digital tools such as IoT-enabled inventory management, AI-driven demand forecasting, integrated customer feedback mechanisms, and transparent sustainability tracking, businesses can overcome these challenges and build resilient, customer-centric, and environmentally responsible operations.

The proposed framework and prototype dashboards demonstrate how digital transformation can translate into tangible outcomes: improved operational efficiency, stronger consumer trust, and measurable contributions to sustainability goals. Importantly, these systems align with the UAE's Green Agenda 2030 and global commitments to responsible consumption, positioning enterprises to thrive in both local and international markets. While challenges such as workforce readiness, system integration, and cost considerations remain, the long-term benefits of agility, transparency, and sustainable growth far outweigh the risks. Ultimately, an intelligent and sustainable supply chain is not just an enabler of competitiveness in smart retail, it is a cornerstone for future-ready enterprises in the UAE.

13. Acknowledgement

The language in this playbook was refined and enhanced using generative AI tools to improve clarity, grammar, and phrasing. All core ideas, structure, content development, and research were conducted and written by the authors. No entire chapters were AI-generated.

14. References

Gomstyn, A., & Jonker, A. (2024, September 30). *Exploring privacy issues in the age of AI*. IBM. https://www.ibm.com/think/insights/ai-privacy

Hadjielias, E., Dada, O. L., & Eliades, K. (2021). *Entrepreneurial process in international multiunit franchise outlets: A social capital perspective*. Journal of Business Research, 134, 13–28. https://doi.org/10.1016/j.jbusres.2021.05.022

Nguyen, K. (2025, January 10). *Ultimate guide to supply chain and operations management 2025*. World's #1 POS for Magento. https://www.magestore.com/blog/operations-and-supply-chain-management/

Reichheld, F. (2003). *The One Number You Need to Grow*. Harvard Business Review. https://www.nashc.net/wp-content/uploads/2014/10/the-one-number-you-need-to-know.pdf

Sarmah, T., (2024) *Exploring the Intersection of Sustainability and Cultural Dynamics in the UAE Fashion Industry: A Literary Review* (December 03, 2024). International Journal of Management and Humanities, volume 11, issue 4, 2024[10.35940/ijmh.D1774.11041224], Available at SSRN: https://ssrn.com/abstract=5072282 or http://dx.doi.org/10.2139/ssrn.5072282

Saxena, A,. & Fernandes, K., (2025) *Transforming UAE's Supply Chain Management through Artificial Intelligence: Case Studies and Insights* (August 15, 2025). Available at SSRN: https://ssrn.com/abstract=5411263 or http://dx.doi.org/10.2139/ssrn.5411263

Seuring, S., & Müller, M. (2008). From a Literature Review to a Conceptual Framework for Sustainable Supply Chain Management. Journal of

Cleaner Production, 16(15), 1699–1710. https://doi.org/10.1016/j.jclepro.2008.04.020

Slack, N., Brandon-Jones, A., & Burgess, N. (2022). *Operations Management* (10th ed.). Pearson.

Tracteck. (2025). Digital Transformation in the UAE: Why Tracking Technologies Are Essential in 2025 and Beyond. https://tracteck.com/digital-transformation-in-the-uae-why-tracking-technologies-are-essential-in-2025-and-beyond-2/

Tsidulko, J. (2024, January 11). Benefits of AI in the Supply Chain. Oracle. https://www.oracle.com/ae/scm/ai-supply-chain/

UAE Government. (2024, May 7). *The UAE's Green Agenda - 2030*. Official Portal of the UAE Government. https://u.ae/en/about-the-uae/strategies-initiatives-and-awards/strategies-plans-and-visions/environment-and-energy/the-uaes-green-agenda-2030

Vinculum Group. (2024). Retail & Fashion Industry in UAE: Growth, Challenges & Solutions. https://www.vinculumgroup.com/retail-fashion-industry-in-uae-growth-challenges-solutions/

SECTION II
MARKET-FIRST APPROACH

Chapter 3

Building a Conscious Commerce Engine: A Smart IS Framework for a UAE-based eco-friendly fashion marketplace

Taha Shabbir Hussain . Akhil Anil Kumar . Maryam Elgamil

Abstract

Sustainable fashion is growing quickly, yet small and medium enterprises (SMEs) face ongoing challenges including low conversion rates, vendor management bottlenecks, and limited transparency of environmental impact. In the UAE's fast-growing e-commerce sector, these issues are particularly pressing for multi-vendor platforms that must coordinate across diverse partners while meeting the expectations of conscious consumers. This chapter examines these challenges through the lens of a UAE-based sustainable fashion marketplace and introduces the Conscious Commerce Engine as a smart information systems (IS) solution. The proposed framework integrates analytics, automation, artificial intelligence, and sustainability tracking to streamline vendor operations, improve customer engagement, and quantify environmental outcomes in real time. By leveraging accessible tools such as Google Analytics 4, BigQuery, Power BI, and blockchain, SMEs can gain enterprise-grade capabilities without prohibitive costs. Aligned with the United Nations Sustainable Development Goals, the Conscious Commerce Engine offers a replicable pathway for SMEs to achieve both competitiveness and environmental responsibility.

Keywords

Sustainable fashion, multi-vendor marketplaces, information systems, digital transformation, sustainability tracking

Taha Shabbir Hussain ✉
University of Wollongong in Dubai
tsh040@uowmail.edu.au

Akhil Anil Kumar
University of Wollongong in Dubai

Maryam Elgamil
University of Wollongong in Dubai

Hussain, T. S., Kumar, A. A., & Elgamil, M. (2025). Building a Conscious Commerce Engine: A Smart IS Framework for a UAE-based eco-friendly fashion marketplace. In Z. R. Khan, P. Bhagwat, P. Mukala, & N. Ruxwana (Eds.), *Technology adoption playbook for sustainability-focused startups and SMEs* (pp. 61-77). ENAI WG Centre for Academic Integrity in the UAE; University of Wollongong in Dubai; Gulf Book Services LTD, UK.

1. Introduction

The rapid growth of sustainable fashion has created both opportunities and challenges for small and medium enterprises (SMEs). Globally, the sustainable fashion market is projected to expand from approximately $8 billion in 2024 to more than four times that size by 2033, driven by consumer demand for environmentally responsible practices (Custom Market Insights, 2024). In the UAE, the e-commerce sector is also experiencing significant growth, with revenues expected to surpass $770 billion by 2033, creating fertile ground for eco-friendly fashion start-ups to scale and innovate (IMARC Group, 2024). However, without the right digital infrastructure, many SMEs struggle with operational inefficiencies, weak customer conversion, and limited sustainability transparency (Li, 2025).

This chapter examines how a UAE-based sustainable fashion marketplace can address these challenges by integrating a smart information systems (IS) framework. The framework leverages advanced technologies such as analytics, automation, and sustainability tracking to optimize vendor management, enhance customer journeys, and provide transparent environmental impact metrics. By aligning commercial innovation with sustainability imperatives, the proposed solution not only improves organizational performance but also contributes to the wider transformation of sustainable fashion into a mainstream retail model.

2. Industry Context

In this chapter, sustainable fashion and ready-made garment SMEs in the UAE are examined. The discussion highlights common industry challenges identified through research and collaboration with businesses in the sector, with the aim of presenting lessons that can be adapted across the wider sustainable commerce landscape.

Business Type: Retail – Sustainable Fashion Marketplace

Sustainable fashion is no longer fringe; it's fast becoming part of everyday retail. Analysts estimate the global market at approximately $8 billion in 2024 and predict it will more than quadruple by 2033, growing at over 20 percent annually (Custom Market Insights, 2024). Closer to home, the UAE's always-online shoppers are leaning in even harder. Local e-commerce clocked roughly $125 billion last year and could surge past $770 billion by 2033 (IMARC Group, 2024). Those kinds of numbers give eco-fashion start-ups room to test bold ideas and scale at speed.
Reality is, however, messier. Small marketplaces handle dozens of vendors, verify ethical claims, and keep prices honest - all on lean budgets. Without

the right tech stack, that complexity becomes overwhelming, and bigger brands with deeper pockets end up winning the race (Li, 2025).

Key business functions most affected by digital transformation include:
- Supply Chain and Operations
- Customer Experience and Feedback
- Sustainability Monitoring
- E-commerce and Sales

3. Business Challenge – pain points

Sustainable e-commerce platforms face a critical paradox: achieving substantial web traffic while struggling with conversion optimization and operational efficiency. This chapter examines UAE-based ethical fashion marketplaces that may be experiencing the following four interconnected challenges, which limit scalability and market impact.

- The Conversion Paradox: Despite generating thousands of monthly website visits, platforms may suffer from persistently low conversion rates. High traffic volumes often fail to translate into proportional sales, indicating fundamental gaps in customer experience and engagement strategies (Saleem et al., 2019)
- Vendor Management Bottlenecks: Managing hundreds of merchant partners can create significant operational friction (Global Market Insights, 2024). Poor communication protocols may lead to delayed responses, missed orders, and delivery delays ranging from two to four days. These operational inefficiencies adversely impact customer satisfaction and compromise the brand's reputation.
- Sustainability Transparency Gap: While environmental impact constitutes a platform's core value proposition, customers may lack visibility into their individual contributions towards sustainability goals. The absence of real-time impact metrics not only undermines the brand's differentiation strategy but also failed to engage environmentally conscious consumers (Market.us, 2024).
- Fragmented Customer Intelligence: The platform operated without comprehensive customer journey mapping and behavioural analytics (Hilal et al., 2025; McGuirk, 2023). This visibility gap prevented personalized marketing, targeted product recommendations, and data-driven decision-making which are essential factors for sustainable growth.

These challenges, which are common among resource-constrained Small and Medium Enterprises (SMEs) in the sustainable commerce sector, demands an integrated information systems approach to unlock operational efficiency and competitive advantage.

4. Proposed Solution Overview

The digital transformation challenge for sustainable SMEs demands a strategic approach that balances operational sophistication with financial pragmatism. Rather than constructing isolated technological silos or pursuing prohibitively expensive custom development, this solution framework embraces an integration-first philosophy that leverages best-of-breed off-the-shelf technologies.

Integral to this IS architecture is compliance with the UAE's Federal Decree-Law No. 45 of 2021 on the Protection of Personal Data (PDPL), which requires robust data security measures, including encryption for personal data at rest and in transit, to safeguard processing activities across interconnected systems (UAE Government, 2021). This ensures lawful data handling, consent acquisition, minimization, and breach notification, aligning with privacy-by-design principles (UAE Data Office, 2021)

The proposed solution centres on four interconnected engines that collectively transform fragmented business operations into a data-driven enterprise:

- Firstly, the Vendor Intelligence Engine works with merchant relationship management by automating onboarding processes, performance tracking protocols, and establishing intelligent communication workflows that eliminate the chronic multi-day delivery delays plaguing multi-vendor platforms.
- Secondly, the Customer Journey Engine addresses the conversion paradox by mapping every digital touchpoint, behavioural nuances, and transforming anonymous website traffic into actionable customer intelligence. This systematic approach converts the platform's visitors from passive browsers into engaged brand advocates.
- The third engine, the Sustainability Engine operationalizes environmental impact transparency by capturing real-time sustainability metrics and presenting them as compelling customer-facing narratives.
- Finally, the Intelligence Engine synthesizes demand forecasting, trend analysis, and competitive pricing intelligence into unified Power BI dashboards, creating a single source of truth that aligns marketing, operations, and financial decision-making.

5. Technologies Involved

The proposed technology stack enables SMEs to orchestrate enterprise-grade capabilities through the strategic integration of accessible cloud-based solutions. As shown in Figure 1, Google Analytics dashboards provide real-time visibility into customer traffic and behaviour patterns, enabling SMEs to track engagement across markets and translate raw data into actionable insights.

5.1. Core Analytics & Intelligence Layer:

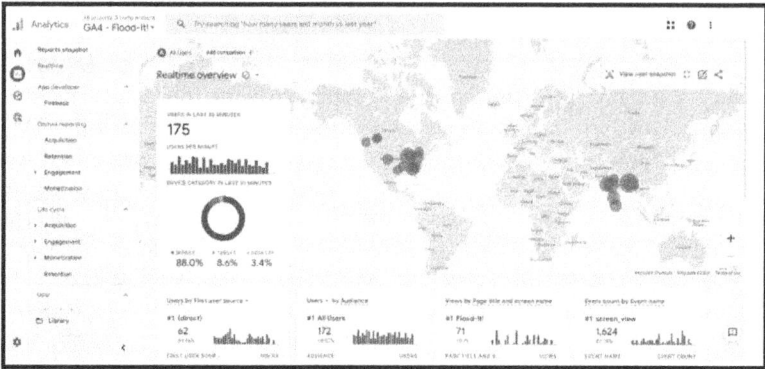

Figure 1: Google Analytics Dashboard (Source: developed by authors as a sample)

- **Google Analytics 4 + BigQuery**: Customer journey tracking with scalable, cost-effective data warehousing for behavioural pattern analysis (Google, 2025a; Google Cloud, 2025; Microsoft, 2025a; Ali et al., 2021). The Google Analytic dashboard, exemplified in Figure 1 as a sample generated by the authors, showcases key performance indicators (KPIs) such as user traffic trends (e.g., 175 users in the last 30 minutes), device category distribution (e.g., 88% mobile, 8.6% tablet, 3.4% desktop), and top traffic sources. Visuals like world maps highlight geographic engagement, while bar charts and pie charts indicate audience growth and event counts (e.g., 1,624 views), derived from real-time Google Analytics 4 data integrated with BigQuery. These KPIs are updated hourly to reflect dynamic market shifts, supporting the Intelligence Engine's demand forecasting and trend analysis.
- **Microsoft Power BI**: Unified dashboard creation, transforming raw data into actionable business intelligence across all operational domains (Microsoft, 2025a; Becker & Gould, 2019).

64

- **Custom Sustainability Tracker Widget**: Real-time environmental impact calculation and display integration based on basic Python

5.2. Operational Automation Backbone:

- **Asana + WhatsApp Business API**: Automated vendor communication workflows eliminating manual order processing bottlenecks
- **HubSpot CRM + Zapier**: Seamless customer data integration with the existing CS-Cart e-commerce platform for 360-degree customer visibility
- **Price2Spy**: Automated competitive pricing intelligence for dynamic market positioning

5.3. AI-Powered Enhancement Suite:

- **ChatGPT API + Canva + Heygen**: Automated, personalized marketing content generation, reducing creative resource requirements
- **Hootsuite Insights + TweetDeck**: social media trend analysis feeding predictive product recommendation algorithms
- **Machine Learning Predictive Analytics**: Demand forecasting models optimizing inventory and marketing resource allocation

5.4. Future-Ready Capabilities:

- **AR/VR Integration Framework**: Enhanced customer experience technologies prepared for scalable implementation (Kumar, 2024; Badhwar et al., 2023)
- **Blockchain Traceability Infrastructure**: Supply chain transparency tools for advanced sustainability verification

Figure 2 illustrates the integrated system architecture for the Conscious Commerce Engine, showing how analytics, automation, AI, and sustainability tools connect into a unified framework to support SMEs' digital transformation.

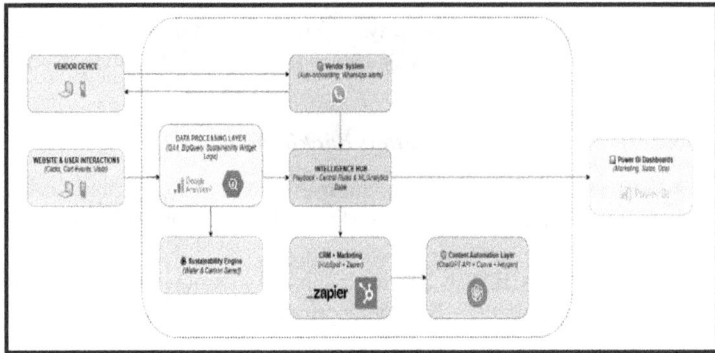

Figure 2: Integrated system architecture for the Conscious Commerce Engine (Source: developed by authors as sample)[1]

Table 1: Data Transformations in the Conscious Commerce Engine (Source: proposed by authors)

Data Element	Source	Transformation	Destination	Update Frequency
Vendor Onboarding Data (e.g., material types, certifications)	Vendor Device	Verification and standardization via WhatsApp alerts	Sustainability Engine, Intelligence Hub	Daily
User Interaction Logs (e.g., clicks, cart events)	Website & User Interactions	Aggregated into behavioural segments using GA4 algorithms	Data Processing Layer, CRM - Marketing	Real-time

---

[1] *Note: Icons reproduced (unaltered) from Google Brand Resource Center - Google Analytics 4 (Google, 2025b) and BigQuery (Google Cloud, 2025); HubSpot App Partner Branding Guidelines - HubSpot (2025); Meta Platforms - WhatsApp Brand Guidelines (2025); Microsoft Power Platform Icons - Power BI (2025b); OpenAI Brand Guidelines - ChatGPT (2025); and Zapier Integration Branding Guidelines - Zapier (2025). Logos © their respective trademark owners; used under fair use for educational and illustrative purposes only and do not imply endorsement.*

Raw Sustainability Metrics (e.g., water usage, carbon emissions)	Vendor Device	Calculated into savings (LCA-based) via Sustainability Widget	Sustainability Engine, Power BI Dashboards	Hourly
Customer Profiles	CRM - Marketing (HubSpot)	Enriched with Zapier integrations for 360-degree views	Content Automation Layer	Daily
Demand Forecasts	Intelligence Hub	Synthesized via ML playbooks	Power BI Dashboards	Hourly
Marketing KPIs	Content Automation Layer	Generated content metrics (e.g., engagement rates)	Power BI Dashboards	Daily

6. Data Use & Analytics

Key Analytics Techniques Employed:

- **Funnel Analysis**: Customer journey mapping through conversion stages
- **Behavioural Segmentation**: Customer clustering based on interaction patterns
- **Performance Benchmarking**: Vendor efficiency tracking and comparative analysis
- **Real-time Impact Calculation**: Environmental metrics aggregation and visualization
- **Predictive Modelling:** Demand forecasting through historical data patterns

The proposed analytics framework closes key data gaps in sustainable fashion marketplaces using evidence-based methods from e-commerce research. Funnel analysis maps the customer journey step by step, showing where visitors drop off and directly addressing the conversion challenge of high traffic but low sales.

67

- *Customer Journey Intelligence*
  Google Analytics 4 enables detailed tracking of customer behaviour, supporting personalized marketing strategies (Hilal et al., 2025). Combined with machine learning, it predicts purchasing patterns and converts anonymous visitors into defined segments, allowing targeted campaigns based on preferences and browsing habits (McGuirk, 2023).
- *Vendor Performance Analytics*
  Efficient vendor management is essential for reducing delays and ensuring supply chain quality (Global Market Insights, 2025). BigQuery supports large-scale analysis of vendor response times, order accuracy, and communication effectiveness across merchant networks (Miryala & Gupta, 2023). Vendor performance metrics, such as on-time delivery rate (>95% target) and order fulfilment accuracy (>98%), are derived from multi-attribute decision-making models in supplier evaluation literature and industry standards. Assumptions include proportional risk-based scaling for SMEs, drawing from B2B e-commerce regressions showing logistics capability impacts (Chen et al., 2021)
- *Sustainability Impact Measurement*
  Real-time sustainability metrics are derived from vendor-reported data on raw materials, production processes, and certifications. Vendors are required to submit details on material types (e.g., cotton varieties) and supporting documentation during onboarding. Submitted information is verified for authenticity and are computed based on standardized emission and resource-use factors for each fabric type. These metrics are then aggregated and visualized in Power BI dashboards, providing transparent, auditable sustainability narratives that support marketplace differentiation and reduce greenwashing risks.

7. Benefits

The transformative potential of integrated information systems extends beyond immediate operational improvements, creating cascading benefits that reshape both organizational capabilities and industry positioning within the sustainable fashion ecosystem.

7.1. Operational Excellence and Revenue Enhancement

The implementation of comprehensive analytics and automation systems directly addresses the conversion optimization challenge plaguing multi-vendor sustainable marketplaces. Research indicates that global e-commerce conversion rates generally range between 2% and 4%, while fashion and apparel retail specifically achieves lower benchmarks, averaging between 1.6% and 1.9%, with some recent datasets reporting values as low as 1.4% (Chaffey, 2025; IRP Commerce, 2025). Customer journey mapping implementations have been shown to deliver conversion improvements through targeted personalization (Saleem et al., 2019). Moreover, marketing strategies that align with sustainability and ESG principles are associated with stronger long-term customer loyalty and lifetime value, even if the precise uplift in customer lifetime value (CLV) from visible environmental metrics is not yet consistently quantified in the literature (Ali and Shabn, 2024). Vendor enhancements could yield 15–20% supply chain efficiency gains, assuming 5–10% initial costs (Schulze et al., 2016)

7.2. Strategic Market Positioning

The sustainability tracking system creates measurable differentiation within an increasingly conscious marketplace. Traditional fashion market's sustainable activities have a positive effect on brand image, trust, and satisfaction. Moreover, they have a positive influence on building brand loyalty (Market.us, 2024).

7.3. Industry-Wide Implications

This integrated approach addresses systemic challenges within sustainable fashion marketplaces, creating scalable solutions applicable across the sector. Corporate goals can bring a large shift in the supply chain, which could pay dividends in raising their business profile and building customer loyalty (Singh, 2025). The proposed framework demonstrates how SMEs can leverage sophisticated technologies to compete effectively against larger retailers while maintaining operational efficiency and environmental accountability. The cumulative impact extends beyond individual organizational benefits, contributing to the broader transformation of sustainable fashion from niche market to mainstream preference through enhanced customer experiences and operational transparency.

8. Risks & Considerations

The implementation of the Conscious Commerce Engine for the UAE-based sustainable fashion marketplace may present specific challenges requiring targeted mitigation strategies.

8.1. Vendor Intelligence Engine Risks

A marketplace's 100+ merchants may face adoption barriers, with vendors who "don't check email" or "don't answer their phone". Key risks include:

- WhatsApp Business API rate limiting during peak periods
- Resistance to Asana workflow integration
- Language barriers requiring Arabic/English support

8.2. Data Integration Vulnerabilities

Multi-platform integration (12+ systems) may create specific failure points:

- Zapier automation breaking from API changes
- HubSpot-CS Cart synchronization delays
- BigQuery downtime cascading across all engines
- Power BI lag processing real-time sustainability metrics

8.3. Sustainability Verification Challenges

The platform may face concerns over verifying sustainability claims from merchants lacking formal certifications. These risks greenwashing accusations and credibility damage.

8.4. Scalability Bottlenecks and Infrastructure Limitations

Scalability remains a central concern for multi-vendor e-commerce platforms, as high traffic can degrade CS-Cart performance without caching and load balancing (CS-Cart Review, 2023). Similarly, data pipelines face constraints; for instance, GA4 with BigQuery enforces daily export caps, creating risks of data loss or latency in real-time reporting (Google, 2023).

8.5. API Integration Vulnerabilities

Reliance on third-party APIs introduces systemic risks, as downtime, rate limits, and version deprecations can cascade into failures across dependent services (Facebook for Developers, 2023). For instance, the WhatsApp Business API enforces strict throughput caps, while HubSpot and Google enforce request limits, necessitating throttling mechanisms and fallback workflows to maintain operational continuity.

8.6. Mitigation Approach

Phased rollout prioritizing high-impact integrations, parallel manual processes during transition, and vendor support during onboarding address these risks (Morić et al., 2024).

9. Evaluation Criteria

Success measurement encompasses both quantitative performance indicators and qualitative transformation metrics. Primary KPIs include conversion rate improvements from baseline traffic analytics, vendor response time reduction from current two-four-day delays, and customer engagement metrics through sustainability impact tracking utilization. Vendor metrics, such as response time (<24 hours) and on-time delivery (>95%), are evaluated using fuzzy multi-attribute models from supplier selection studies, assuming AHP weighting and benchmarks from e-commerce cases with 15–20% efficiency gains (Awasthi et al., 2015; Schulze et al., 2016).

Revenue optimization indicators measure personalized marketing campaign effectiveness, demand forecasting accuracy rates, and inventory turnover improvements. Operational efficiency metrics track vendor onboarding time reduction, automated communication response rates, and customer service resolution speeds.

Sustainability impact assessment evaluates environmental metric accuracy, customer engagement with impact data, and brand differentiation effectiveness within the ethical fashion marketplace. Real-time sustainability metrics are derived from vendor-reported data on raw materials (e.g., cotton varieties), production processes, and adherence to recognized environmental standards, verified during onboarding to ensure authenticity and reduce greenwashing risks (Suryawanshi & Dutta, 2022). Environmental impact calculations, including water usage, carbon footprint, and waste generation, are computed using standardized life cycle assessment (LCA) factors for fabrics, aggregated, and visualized in Power BI dashboards for transparent, auditable narratives (McKinsey & Company, 2024). Long-term success indicators include market share growth, customer retention rates, and funding acquisition facilitated by demonstrable operational improvements and measurable sustainability outcomes.

10. Sustainability Alignment

The proposed framework promises to enhance UAE-based eco-friendly fashion marketplaces by aligning digital innovation with sustainability, improving efficiency, and environmental impact, with key alignments in:

- The system tracks water use, carbon emissions, and waste reduction in real time, turning abstract sustainability goals into measurable results.
- By selecting vendors with verified environmental credentials and efficient logistics, the platform fosters sustainable practices and lowers emissions.
- Real-time impact data links purchases to environmental outcomes, encouraging informed choices, loyalty, and advocacy.
- The model advances SDG 12 and SDG 13 by enabling transparent supply chains and promoting sustainable fashion consumption

11. Conclusion

This chapter has shown how sustainable fashion SMEs in the UAE can overcome critical barriers, low conversion rates, vendor inefficiencies, transparency gaps, and fragmented customer intelligence, through the Conscious Commerce Engine. The Conscious Commerce Engine is designed as a replicable framework, allowing SMEs across regions to integrate analytics, automation, and sustainability tracking in resource-efficient ways by integrating analytics, automation, and sustainability tracking into a unified framework, the model demonstrates how SMEs can achieve operational efficiency and measurable environmental impact while competing in a rapidly expanding digital marketplace.

Beyond addressing immediate challenges, the proposed framework establishes a scalable, replicable pathway for SMEs globally. Its alignment with the United Nations Sustainable Development Goals underscores how profitability and environmental responsibility can reinforce each other. In doing so, the Conscious Commerce Engine promises to not only strengthen organizational performance but also contributes to the broader transformation of sustainable fashion from niche concept to mainstream retail model.

12. References

Ali, M.H., Hosain, M.S. & Hossain, M.A., (2021). Big Data analysis using BigQuery on cloud computing platform. *Australian Journal of Engineering and Innovative Technology*, 3(1), pp.1-9.

Ali, N., & Shabn, O. S. (2024). Customer lifetime value (CLV) insights for strategic marketing success and its impact on organizational financial performance. *Cogent Business & Management*, *11*(1). https://doi.org/10.1080/23311975.2024.2361321

Awasthi, A., Govindan, K., & Goldbeck, G. S. (2015). Multi-tier sustainable global supplier selection using fuzzy TOPSIS. International Journal of Production Economics, 166, 11–21.

Badhwar, A., Islam, S., & Tan, C. S. L. (2023). Exploring the potential of blockchain technology within the fashion and textile supply chain with a focus on traceability, transparency, and product authenticity: A systematic review. Frontiers in Blockchain, 6, Article 1044723. https://doi.org/10.3389/fbloc.2023.1044723

Becker, L.T. & Gould, E.M., (2019). Microsoft Power BI: Extending Excel to Manipulate, Analyze, and Visualize Diverse Data. *Serials Review*, *45*(3), 184–188. https://doi.org/10.1080/00987913.2019.1644891

Chaffey, D. (2025, January 2). *E-commerce conversion rate benchmarks – 2025 update.* Smart Insights.

https://www.smartinsights.com/ecommerce/ecommerce-analytics/ecommerce-conversion-rates/

Chen, J., Liu, X., & Li, Y. (2021). The impact of logistics capability on e-commerce performance: An empirical study. Journal of Business Research, 125, 456–467.

CS-Cart Review. (2023). *Unlock the full potential of CS-Cart*. Retrieved from https://www.cscart.com

Custom Market Insights. (2024). *Global Sustainable Fashion Market 2024–2033: Sustainable Fashion Market Size, Trends and Insights* [Industry report]. Custom Market Insights. https://www.custommarketinsights.com/report/sustainable-fashion-market/

Facebook for Developers. (2023). *WhatsApp Business Platform: Cloud API overview.* Retrieved from https://developers.facebook.com/docs/whatsapp/cloud-api/overview

Global Market Insights. (2025, March). Sustainable clothing market – By type, by material, by price range, by end use, by distribution channel – Global forecast, 2025–2034 [Report ID: GMI10224]. GMInsights. https://www.gminsights.com/industry-analysis/sustainable-clothing-market Global Market Insights Inc.

Google. (2023). *Export Google Analytics 4 data to BigQuery*. Google Help. Retrieved from https://support.google.com/analytics/answer/9823238

Google. (2025a). *[GA4] Introducing the next generation of Analytics, Google Analytics 4*. Google Analytics Help Center. Retrieved July 30, 2025, from https://support.google.com/analytics/answer/10089681

Google. (2025b). *Brand Resource Center: Product icon guidelines*. https://about.google/brand-resource-center/brand-elements/

Google Cloud. (2025). *BigQuery documentation*. Retrieved July 30, 2025, from https://cloud.google.com/bigquery/docs

Hilal, M., Sumbal, & Imad, M. (2025). Strategic Imperative of Data Analytics: Empowering Informed Business Decision-Making. In: Arezki, S., Ouaissa, M., Ouaissa, M., Krichen, M., Nayyar, A. (eds) Emerging Disruptive Technologies for Society 5.0 in Developing Countries. Advances in Science, Technology & Innovation. Springer, Cham. https://doi.org/10.1007/978-3-031-63701-8_6

HubSpot. (2025). *App partner branding guidelines*. https://www.hubspot.com/partners/app/branding-guidelines

IMARC Group. (2024). *UAE E-Commerce Market Size, Share, Trends Report, 2033* [Market analysis]. **Report ID:** SR112025A23477. IMARC Group. https://www.imarcgroup.com/uae-e-commerce-market

IRP Commerce. (2025, August). *Clothing & accessories ecommerce market data.* https://www.irpcommerce.com/en/gb/ecommercemarketdata. aspx?Market=3

Kumar, A. (2024, October 3). *Augmented reality and virtual reality: Reimagining try-before-you-buy.* Retail Customer Experience. https://www.retailcustomerexperience.com/blogs/augmented-reality-and-virtual-reality-reimagining-try-before-you-buy/

Li, J. (2025). Challenges and strategies for SMEs in the apparel industry: Navigating technological and sustainable transformations. In *Proceedings of the 1st International Conference on Modern Logistics and Supply Chain Management (MLSCM 2024)* (pp. 457–460). SciTePress. https://doi.org/10.5220/0013337900004558

Market.us. (2024, December). Global sustainable fashion market size, share, growth analysis by type (Tops and T-Shirts, Pants and Trousers, Jeans and Denim, Shorts and Skirts, Sweaters, Swimsuits, Others), by material (Organic Cotton, Recycled Fabrics, Eco-friendly Dyes, Hemp, Bamboo, Others), by price range, by end user, by distribution channel, by region and companies – Industry segment outlook, market assessment, competition scenario, statistics, trends and forecast 2024–2033 [Report ID: 136204]. Market.us. https://market.us/report/sustainable-fashion-market/ Market.us

McKinsey & Company. (2024). Sustainable style: How fashion can afford and accelerate decarbonization. https://www.mckinsey.com/industries/retail/our-insights/sustainable-style-how-fashion-can-afford-and-accelerate-decarbonization

Singh, S. (2025, May). *Sustainable fashion market report 2025 (Global Edition)* [Report ID: CMR963954]. Cognitive Market Research. https://www.cognitivemarketresearch.com/sustainable-fashion-market-report

McGuirk, M. (2023) Performing web analytics with Google Analytics 4: a platform review. *J Market Anal* **11**, 854–868 (2023). https://doi.org/10.1057/s41270-023-00244-4

Meta. (2025). *WhatsApp brand guidelines: Proper logo and branding usage.* https://www.infobip.com/docs/whatsapp/compliance/brand-guidelines

Microsoft. (2025a). *What is Power BI? Overview of components and benefits.* Microsoft Learn. https://learn.microsoft.com/en-us/power-bi/fundamentals/power-bi-overview

Microsoft. (2025b, May 29). *Microsoft Power Platform icons.* https://learn.microsoft.com/en-us/power-platform/guidance/icons

Miryala, N. K., & Gupta, D. (2023). Big data analytics in cloud: Comparative study. *International Journal of Computer Trends and Technology, 71*(12), 30–34. Big Data Analytics in Cloud – Comparative Study

Morić, Z., Đakić, V., Đekić, D., & Regvart, D. (2024). Protection of personal data in the context of e-commerce. *Journal of Cybersecurity and Privacy, 4*(3), 731–761. https://doi.org/10.3390/jcp4030034

OpenAI. (2025). *Design guidelines.* https://openai.com/brand/

Saleem, H., Uddin, M. K. S., Habib-ur-Rehman, *et al.* (2019). Strategic data driven approach to improve conversion rates and sales performance of e-commerce websites. *International Journal of Scientific & Engineering Research, 10*(4), 588-593. https://www.semanticscholar.org/paper/Strategic-Data-Driven-Approach-to-Improve-Rates-and-Saleem-Khawaja/0172d9c9ab93dd3bbbd397a28d76def198bc48d1

Schulze, H., Bals, L., & Johnsen, T. E. (2016). Varieties and interdependencies of supplier-induced risks and contingencies in sourcing. Supply Chain Management: An International Journal, 21(5), 655–672. https://doi.org/10.1108/SCM-02-2016-0045

Suryawanshi, P., & Dutta, P. (2022). Designing sustainable supply chain metrics for the Indonesian fashion industry: A DEMATEL-based ANP approach. Sustainable Operations and Computers, 3, 149–159.

UAE Data Office. (2021). *Personal Data Protection Law.* The Official Portal of the UAE Government. Retrieved October 3, 2025, from https://u.ae/en/about-the-uae/digital-uae/data/data-protection-laws

Zapier. (2025). *Integration branding guidelines.* https://docs.zapier.com/platform/publish/branding-guidelines

SECTION III
CUSTOMER-FIRST APPROACH

Chapter 4

Next-Gen CRMs for SMEs: Enhancing Customer Engagement with RAP Plugins

Nigel Noronha . Raphael Dypiangco . Frenica D'souza . Nathan Matthew

Abstract

Small and medium-sized enterprises (SMEs) in the UAE such as sustainable fashion marketplaces face rising pressure to deliver fast, transparent, and reliable customer service while competing against larger omni-channel retailers. Yet many still rely on fragmented tools such as spreadsheets, emails, and social media chats, which slow responses, complicate supplier management, and erode customer trust. This chapter proposes a modular solution that layers Reusable Automation and Processing (RAP) plugins onto a cloud-based CRM to unify operations. Drawing on national digital strategies, industry studies, and sector-specific examples, it outlines a phased 12-week implementation roadmap and a reference architecture designed for scalability and low risk. Benefits include measurable efficiency gains, reduced errors, and greater capacity, supported by evaluation criteria and risk mitigation strategies. By integrating automation, intelligence, and secure data practices, RAP-enhanced CRMs offer sustainable fashion SMEs a pathway to improved competitiveness, stronger customer relationships, and alignment with the UAE's vision for digital transformation and responsible growth.

Keywords

Sustainable fashion marketplaces, SMEs, CRM, automation, UAE digital transformation

Nigel Noronha ✉
University of Wollongong in Dubai
nin740@uowmail.edu.au

Raphael Dypiangco
University of Wollongong in Dubai

Frenica D'souza
University of Wollongong in Dubai

Nathan Matthew
University of Wollongong in Dubai

Noronha, N., Dypiangco, R.., D'souza, F., & Mathew, N (2025). Next-Gen CRMs for SMEs: Enhancing Customer Engagement with RAP Plugins. In Z. R. Khan, P. Bhagwat, P. Mukala, & N. Ruxwana (Eds.), *Technology adoption playbook for sustainability-focused startups and SMEs* (pp. 81-95). ENAI WG Centre for Academic Integrity in the UAE; University of Wollongong in Dubai; Gulf Book Services LTD, UK.

1. Introduction

Running a sustainable clothing marketplace in the UAE comes with unique challenges. While the business promotes eco-friendly choices, its customer management often relies on scattered spreadsheets, email threads, and social media chats. This fragmentation slows responses, complicates supplier tracking, and risks missed opportunities when shoppers switch channels. For a brand built on values of trust and sustainability, these inefficiencies can undermine both credibility and growth (Matsh Consulting, 2025; Gonzalez, 2024)

At the same time, customer expectations in the UAE are rising quickly. Shoppers, especially those seeking sustainable products, expect instant replies on WhatsApp, smooth returns, and transparent updates on deliveries and certifications. Studies show that prospects who wait more than an hour for a response are twice as likely to switch to a competitor (Rep.ai, 2024), while many consumers now define an *"immediate"* reply as 10 minutes or less (Superhuman, 2025). Larger retailers already use omni-channel CRMs and AI-driven service platforms, which puts extra pressure on SMEs to keep up without the same resources.

This chapter explores how a modular, cloud-based CRM enhanced with Reusable Automation and Processing (RAP) plugins can help this kind of sustainable marketplace. By phasing the rollout, starting with a single customer view, then automating key processes, and finally adding predictive intelligence, the marketplace can reduce admin work, improve response times, and build stronger trust with customers. In doing so, it not only enhances efficiency but also aligns with the UAE's Vision 2031 and Digital Government Strategy 2025 goals for innovation and responsible growth (UAE Government, 2023a; 2023b).

2. Industry Context

In this chapter, sustainable clothing marketplace SMEs in the UAE are examined to illustrate the challenges of fragmented customer management systems and the opportunities offered by next-generation CRM solutions. The proposed RAP-enhanced CRM framework responds to common SME pain points identified through research and sectoral case analysis, aiming to present lessons transferable to other small and medium enterprises.

Business Type: Retail – Sustainable Clothing Marketplace

For the UAE, organisations ought to align with projected digital milestones. These are entrenched in Vision 2031 as expectations and set attainable digital targets. The national strategy aims to double GDP to AED 3 trillion and raise non-oil exports to AED 800 billion, with SMEs expected to contribute around 60 per cent of non-oil GDP (UAE Government, 2023a). Complementing this, the UAE Digital Government Strategy 2025 underlines the importance of data-driven decision-making and digital-by-design processes across both public and private sectors (UAE Government, 2023b).

At the same time, customer expectations are rapidly evolving. Residents, expats, and tourists rely heavily on mobile messaging as their primary channel and increasingly demand 24/7 availability, instant quotes, and paperless contracting. Norms such as same-day delivery in e-commerce are spilling over into services and B2B supply chains, setting higher benchmarks for responsiveness across industries.

This transformation also unfolds against the backdrop of multicultural operations. A typical SME employs teams speaking Arabic, English, Hindi or Urdu, and Tagalog, making communication across shifts a challenge. Without a shared timeline, important context can be lost in translation. Multilingual templates, auto-translated quick replies, and clear status flags are becoming essential to ensure continuity and reduce friction.

Competitive urgency further intensifies the picture. More than 94 per cent of UAE companies are SMEs (Matsh Consulting, 2025), yet large regional players already operate omni-channel CRMs and AI-driven service platforms. To avoid market-share erosion, smaller firms need modular solutions that let them adopt comparable capabilities within a quarter, keeping pace with the digital race without shouldering enterprise-level complexity.

Key operational areas typically impacted by CRM-driven digital transformation include:

- Customer Relationship Management and Onboarding
- Multi-channel Communication and Support
- Workflow Automation and Service Efficiency
- Data Integration and Predictive Analytics
- Compliance, Certification, and Sustainability Tracking

3. Business Challenge – pain points

Sustainable online marketplaces in the UAE face distinct challenges in managing customer relationships and supplier operations. Reliance on fragmented, manual systems undermines both efficiency and growth. The challenges may include:

- Customer and supplier data spread across email threads, Excel sheets, and social media chats, creating duplication and delays.
- Without CRM automation for e-signatures and expiry tracking, staff chase contracts and certificates manually, slowing compliance and approvals.
- Inquiries from Instagram, WhatsApp, and web chat are re-keyed, causing context loss when shoppers switch channels.
- Even simple tasks like issuing a return label take 15 minutes, turning routine processes into costly bottlenecks.
- Five staff spending 30 minutes daily hunting data or paperwork could lose 11 hours weekly, estimated at over AED 65,000 annually at AED 120 per hour. Automation could cut routine labour costs by 30% (Matsh Consulting, 2025; Gonzalez, 2024).
- Prospects waiting over an hour for a reply are twice as likely to defect (Rep.ai, 2024). With 82% of consumers, including UAE WhatsApp users, expecting replies quickly (D7 Networks, 2025), halving reply times can increase conversions by 10–15% (NobelBiz, 2024).
- Single-purpose apps collapse under multichannel demands, while large on-premises CRMs require costly rollouts and training, often abandoned before results appear.

4. Proposed Solution

A proposed **Reusable Automation and Processing (RAP) plugin** strategy layers on a cloud CRM to create an integrated customer-operations hub. Five elements can be adopted in phases:

- **CRM core**

   Cloud CRM holds contacts, organisations, opportunities, tickets, and supplier records, replacing disparate spreadsheets while offering role-based permissions, audit trails, and mobile access (SableCRM, 2025).

- **Integration layer (RAP plugins)**

   Self-contained connectors listen for events, normalise payloads, and write them into the CRM. Plugins typically cover WhatsApp Business, Instagram Direct, web chat, email, and forms, then forward clean events to the data warehouse.

- **Automation engine**

   Visual workflows enforce if-then rules and SLAs: send an e-contract when a deal moves to "Proposal," remind clients after 48 hours if unsigned, and trigger high-priority tickets when sentiment analysis flags negative language.

- **Data and intelligence services**

  Microservices add predictive lead scoring (0–100), sentiment detection, and smart routing. Regular retraining prevents model drift and keeps AI systems reliable (Lumenova AI, 2025). In the UAE context, this includes using bilingual data to reflect the market's multilingual environment.

- **Analytics and reporting**

  Dashboards surface KPIs such as average response time, conversion by segment, churn risk, and onboarding cycle length. Managers receive weekly snapshots for early intervention.

4.1. Implementation roadmap

While Sections 4.1–4.5 outlined the core elements of the RAP-enhanced CRM solution, the following roadmap shows how SMEs can phase implementation over 12 weeks to reduce risk and demonstrate quick wins. To address the operational challenges SMEs face with fragmented customer data, sluggish responses, and manual onboarding, a phased approach is essential. Rather than attempting a large-scale transformation at once, this roadmap proposes a 12-week progression: first creating a single source of truth, then building automation to streamline key processes, and finally introducing intelligence for predictive decision-making. Each stage is designed to deliver tangible outcomes quickly, ensuring teams see value early while minimising adoption risks. Table 1 summarises the roadmap, highlighting the phases, weeks, key tasks, and expected outcomes.

Table 1. Phased 12-week implementation roadmap for RAP-enhanced CRM adoption (Source: developed by authors as sample recommendation)

Phase	Weeks	Key tasks	Outcome
Foundation	1–4	CRM set-up, data migration, WhatsApp plugin, core fields	Single customer view; faster replies
Automation	5–8	Email & Instagram plugins,	Paperless onboarding

		workflow templates, e-contract library	
Intelligence	9–12	Lead-score model, sentiment analysis, dashboards, training	Predictive prioritisation

As shown in Table 1, the proposed roadmap begins with establishing a single source of truth (Weeks 1–4), introduces automation to streamline onboarding (Weeks 5–8), and culminates in intelligence-driven decision-making (Weeks 9–12). Each plugin in this architecture subscribes to a webhook, translates payloads into a standard schema, upserts the CRM, logs the activity, triggers automations, and streams an event to the warehouse. Because plugins are stateless and horizontally scalable, new channels can be added without rewriting earlier integrations. This modularity enables SMEs to pilot one high-impact process with low risk, then expand rapidly once early benefits are demonstrated.

4.2. Reference architecture

While the roadmap illustrates when and how SMEs can adopt the solution, the reference architecture explains what underpins it technically. The solution rests on six core components that work together to unify customer data, streamline engagement, and enable intelligence. Each component plays a distinct role but is designed to remain modular, enabling SMEs to adopt incrementally without committing to a heavy enterprise roll-out.

Table 2. Six core components of the RAP-enhanced CRM reference architecture (Source: developed by authors as sample recommendation)

Ref	Component	Purpose	Generic options
4.1	Cloud CRM	Acts as the central customer record, ensuring every	SaaS CRM or open source

		interaction updates a single source of truth and reducing reliance on scattered spreadsheets.	
4.2	RAP plugin SDK	Provides low-code integration that connects new communication channels into the CRM without rewriting existing systems, making expansion low-risk.	REST webhooks, JSON schema
4.3	Communication APIs	Deliver omni-channel messaging so businesses can meet customers on their preferred platforms, from WhatsApp to Instagram, while maintaining context.	WhatsApp Business, SMTP/IMAP, Instagram Messaging

4.4	Workflow engine	Powers visual rules and service-level agreements, turning manual onboarding or follow-up tasks into automated processes that cut delays and errors.	Serverless functions or BPM tools
4.5	Data warehouse + BI	Stores historical interactions and feeds lightweight dashboards, enabling SMEs to track performance, spot bottlenecks, and demonstrate compliance.	Cloud SQL, object storage, lightweight BI
4.6	AI microservices	Add intelligence through lead scoring, sentiment analysis, and predictive models, helping teams prioritise engagement and tailor responses.	Hosted NLP endpoints

5. System Diagram

To visualise how the solution's components interconnect, Figure 1 maps the core layers of the RAP-enhanced CRM. Communication channels feed into the CRM core, which links to integration and automation workflows.

These, in turn, connect to data and intelligence services, with insights surfaced through analytics and reporting tools such as Power BI.

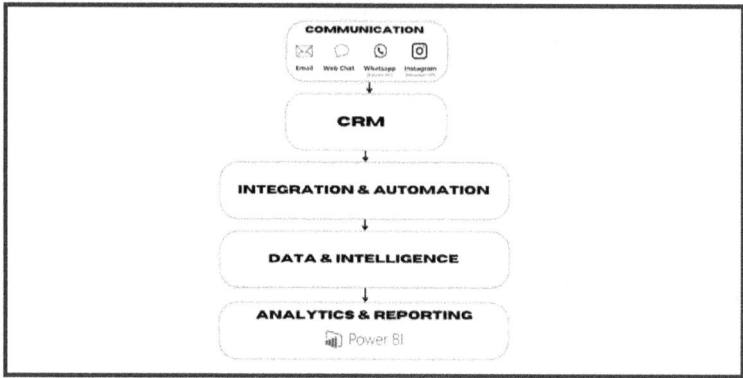

Figure 1. High-level architecture of a RAP-enhanced cloud CRM (Source: developed by authors as sample).

6. Data Collection and Analytics

Data flow: Customer interactions from WhatsApp, Instagram, email, or the website are captured, cleaned, and linked to the right record. The system stores them in a central database, adding details like source, tone, and response time for flexible reporting.

Industry-specific analytics: The system highlights patterns by sector:
- Retail: Remind customers about abandoned carts, track popular products, measure influencer impact.
- Field services: Monitor dispatch times, service feedback, and recurring issues.
- Manufacturing: Forecast certificate expiries, track defects, and spot seasonal trends.
- Data governance: A shared data dictionary defines "lead," "opportunity," and "service ticket." Validation at capture standardises addresses and licence numbers; two-factor authentication and encryption at rest and in transit meet UAE privacy requirements (UAE Government, 2023b).

Actionable insights:
- Marketing reallocates budget to customer segments that respond best to campaigns.
- Operations adjust staffing or workflows when response times begin to slow.

- Finance improves cash flow forecasts by tracking onboarding and order completion dates in real time.

7. Benefits

SMEs in the UAE that adopt automation see measurable wins. Research highlights productivity improvements of up to 30% and error reductions of around 25% (Gonzalez, 2024; Matsh Consulting, 2025), confirming the value of streamlined workflows. Building on this, the proposed RAP rollouts in this chapter illustrate how SMEs could achieve 60% faster replies, 50% less admin during onboarding, and nearly doubled client capacity as cycle times shorten.

Beyond efficiency, the approach also scales easily: adding a new region, channel, or product line requires configuration rather than redevelopment. Over time, the creation of a unified customer timeline becomes a strategic asset, enabling predictive analytics, smoother product launches, compliance audits, and more accurate credit decisions.

Risks and Considerations

Bringing new CRM and automation tools into UAE SMEs comes with risks that need to be managed. Table 2 categorises these risks and provides corresponding mitigation measures:

Table 3: Key risks and mitigation strategies for RAP-enhanced CRM adoption in UAE SMEs (Source: developed by authors as sample)

Category	Risk	Mitigation
Security	Data breach	Encryption, MFA, least-privilege roles, UAE data residency
Integration	Legacy complexity	Pilot one channel, phased migration, sandbox testing
Change management	Low adoption	Role-based training, quick-win dashboards, champion users
Model drift	AI accuracy	Quarterly reviews; retraining with

		bilingual data (Lumenova AI, 2025)
Infrastructure	API limits, webhook failures	Queues, retry logic, correlation IDs
Budget	Usage overruns	Monitor API calls, tiered rollout, cost alerts

8. Evaluation Criteria

Success should be measured with both operational data and feedback from staff and customers. Table 4 translates the proposed measures into evaluation areas, KPIs, and suggested benchmarks, forming a balanced scorecard that reflects both performance and human impact.

Table 4. Proposed Evaluation criteria and suggested benchmarks for RAP-enhanced CRM adoption (Source: developed by authors as sample)

Area	KPI / Measure	Suggested Benchmark (Industry-aligned)
Security	Encryption, multi-factor authentication (MFA), UAE-based storage	100% compliance with UAE Digital Government standards
Integration	Smooth channel onboarding, sandbox testing	≥90% of new channels integrated without major disruption
Adoption	Staff training completion, dashboard use, presence of champion users	≥80% of staff trained and active within 3 months; at least one champion per team
AI Accuracy	Quarterly reviews, bilingual retraining (Zhang, 2024)	Maintain ≥85% model accuracy across languages

Reliability	System uptime, error rates, use of queues/retry logic	≥99% uptime; <1% error rate
Budget Control	API usage monitoring, phased rollouts, cost alerts	Costs remain within ±10% of projected budget
Human Impact	Staff and customer feedback (surveys, NPS, focus groups)	Positive satisfaction trends within first 6 months

9. Sustainability Alignment

Even firms outside traditionally eco-focused sectors now face rising compliance requirements around safety, quality, labour standards, and ESG reporting. In the UAE, these expectations are reinforced by national strategies such as Vision 2031, which emphasises transparency, sustainability, and responsible growth. Regulators, supply-chain partners, and financiers increasingly demand up-to-date documentation as a condition for contracts, partnerships, or credit access. For SMEs, managing these requirements manually through spreadsheets or email threads creates risks of expired certificates, delayed approvals, or missed opportunities.

Automated document tracking offers a practical solution. By keeping certificates current, audit-ready, and instantly shareable, SMEs can respond quickly to regulators, prove compliance to partners, and meet the reporting standards required for green financing. This not only reduces administrative overhead but also strengthens trust with stakeholders and unlocks incentives linked to transparency and ESG alignment. In effect, automation transforms compliance from a costly obligation into a competitive advantage, positioning SMEs as credible contributors to the UAE's sustainability agenda.

Conclusion

This chapter has highlighted how sustainable SMEs in the UAE face persistent challenges when managing customers and suppliers through fragmented spreadsheets, emails, and chats. Rising consumer expectations, national digital strategies, and competitive pressures require these businesses to adopt more integrated solutions. By layering RAP plugins onto a cloud CRM, SMEs can move from manual, reactive operations toward streamlined, data-driven engagement. The phased roadmap and reference architecture presented here demonstrate how implementation can be achieved in manageable steps, reducing risk while showing value early.

The proposed framework goes beyond efficiency gains to offer scalability, resilience, and alignment with the UAE's broader goals for innovation and sustainability. Structured evaluation criteria and risk management approaches ensure adoption remains reliable, secure, and cost-effective, while automated compliance tracking positions SMEs as trusted partners in evolving ESG landscapes. In sum, RAP-enhanced CRMs provide a practical pathway for SMEs to strengthen customer trust, improve competitiveness, and contribute meaningfully to the UAE's vision of responsible digital growth.

10. Acknowledgement

The authors acknowledge the use of generative AI tools, including ChatGPT, to enhance language clarity and succinctness, as well as the editorial guidance and support provided by the faculty supervisor.

11. References

D7 Networks. (2025, July 29). *WhatsApp business statistics you need to know in 2025.* https://d7networks.com/blog/whatsapp-business-statistics/

González, J. (2024, December 18). *How process automation can save time and costs in your SME.* White Wall Software Whitewall-ERS. https://whitewall-ers.com/en/blog/how-process-automation-can-save-time-and-costs-in-your-sme/

Matsh Consulting. (2025, February 18). *Cost-benefit analysis of AI adoption for SMEs in Dubai.* https://www.matsh.co/en/cost-benefit-analysis-of-ai-adoption-for-smes-in-dubai/

Lumenova AI. (2025, February 25). *Model drift: Detecting, preventing and managing model drift.* https://www.lumenova.ai/blog/model-drift-strategies-solutions/

NobelBiz. (2024, May 12). *What is omnichannel customer engagement and how to improve it.* https://nobelbiz.com/blog/what-is-omnichannel-customer-engagement-how-to-improve-it/

Rep.ai. (2024). *9 lead response time statistics.* https://rep.ai/blog/lead-response

SableCRM. (2025). *The benefits of cloud-based CRM solutions for SMEs.* https://www.sablecrm.com/the-benefits-of-cloud-based-crm-solutions-for-small-and-medium-enterprises-smes/

Superhuman. (2025). *Email response time statistics: What businesses need to know.* https://blog.superhuman.com/email-response-time-statistics/

UAE Government. (2023a). *We the UAE 2031 vision.* https://u.ae/en/about-the-uae/strategies-initiatives-and-awards/strategies-plans-and-visions/innovation-and-future-shaping/we-the-uae-2031-vision

UAE Government. (2023b). *UAE Digital Government Strategy 2025.* https://u.ae/en/about-the-uae/strategies-initiatives-and-awards/strategies-plans-and-visions/government-services-and-digital-transformation/uae-national-digital-government-strategy

Chapter 5

Enabling Business Intelligence through Unified CRM Ecosystems

Sara Ranjbar. Farhana Islam . Hawra Virani

Abstract
Small and medium-sized enterprises (SMEs) in the UAE's sustainable consumer goods sector face persistent challenges in managing customer relationships effectively. Many rely on fragmented data systems, manual communication, and limited analytics, which impede scalability and weaken customer loyalty. Drawing on observed industry pain points and student-led analysis, this chapter proposes a unified customer relationship management (CRM) ecosystem powered by business intelligence to address these barriers. The framework integrates key digital platforms, including HubSpot, Shopify, Klaviyo, WhatsApp Business API, Smile.io, and Microsoft Power BI, into a centralized system that consolidates customer data, automates workflows, and provides real-time analytics. This interconnected ecosystem enables behavior-based marketing, gamified loyalty programs, and personalized communication strategies that enhance customer satisfaction and strengthen long-term engagement. The proposed solution highlights benefits such as improved operational efficiency, better customer retention, enhanced data visibility, and greater scalability. At the same time, it acknowledges risks associated with system integration, data privacy, rising costs, and user adoption. By aligning CRM transformation with sustainability values, the chapter demonstrates how UAE-based SMEs can achieve competitive advantage while reinforcing environmentally responsible business practices.

Keywords
CRM ecosystems, business intelligence, sustainable SMEs, customer engagement, UAE e-commerce

---

Sara Ranjbar ✉
University of Wollongong in Dubai
nin740@uowmail.edu.au

Farhana Islam
University of Wollongong in Dubai

Hawra Virani
University of Wollongong in Dubai

Ranjbar, S., Islam, F., & Virani, H. (2025). Enabling Business Intelligence through Unified CRM Ecosystems. In Z. R. Khan, P. Bhagwat, P. Mukala, & N. Ruxwana (Eds.), *Technology adoption playbook for sustainability-focused startups and SMEs* (pp. 97-108). ENAI WG Centre for Academic Integrity in the UAE; University of Wollongong in Dubai; Gulf Book Services LTD, UK.

1. Introduction

Small and medium-sized enterprises (SMEs) in the UAE's sustainable product sector are increasingly recognized as important drivers of eco-conscious consumer markets. However, they face persistent challenges including fragmented customer data, manual communication practices, and limited analytics capacity. Such constraints hinder growth, reduce customer loyalty, and prevent proactive responses to market dynamics. Studies show that CRM adoption among SMEs is often constrained by organizational readiness, digital infrastructure, and workforce skills, which can limit their ability to fully leverage customer data for sustainable growth (Religia et al., 2025).

Research highlights that integrated CRM systems can strengthen SMEs' sustainability performance by enhancing customer orientation, streamlining communication, and embedding knowledge management practices. Evidence from regional contexts indicates that customer orientation, CRM organization, technology integration, and knowledge management significantly improve business sustainability outcomes (Hanaysha et al., 2022). Similarly, studies in the UAE demonstrate that advanced analytics within CRM systems can increase customer satisfaction and decision-making effectiveness, though concerns about ethical data use and privacy remain significant (Morshed, 2024).

At the same time, digital transformation exposes SMEs to risks such as rising operational costs, data security vulnerabilities, and the need for specialized skills. Reports on cloud adoption in the UAE emphasize both opportunities, such as scalability, innovation, and efficiency, and the risks of compliance gaps and security lapses (Access Partnership, 2022). This chapter draws on observed pain points in sustainable SME in the UAE to explore how unified CRM ecosystems, informed by business intelligence and sustainability principles, can enable responsible scaling, customer-centric engagement, and trust-building in the digital era.

2. Industry Context

In this chapter, sustainable product-making SMEs in the UAE are considered as the focal sector. The discussion draws on recurring challenges identified through engagements with businesses, highlighting common pain points in customer relationship management (CRM) and offering insights that can be generalized across the industry.

Business Type: Retail – Sustainable Consumer Goods (E-commerce)

The sustainable consumer goods sector in the UAE, spanning categories such as personal care, home essentials, and eco-friendly fashion, is rapidly expanding in response to rising consumer demand for environmentally responsible choices. These SMEs increasingly rely on e-commerce and digital platforms as their main sales and marketing channels, positioning direct-to-consumer interactions at the heart of their growth strategies.

For enterprises in this space, customer relationship management is emerging as a critical driver of competitiveness and long-term sustainability. Many SMEs struggle with fragmented customer data, manual follow-up processes, and limited capacity to analyze consumer behavior. Such gaps restrict their ability to nurture loyalty and deliver personalized, efficient experiences. Integrating unified CRM ecosystems allows businesses to centralize customer data, automate communication, and align engagement practices with sustainability values. This not only strengthens customer satisfaction but also supports SMEs in scaling responsibly while maintaining their eco-conscious identity.

Key business areas typically impacted by CRM transformation include:

- Customer Experience and Engagement
- Data Analytics and Insights
- Loyalty and Retention Programs
- Marketing Automation and Communication

3. Business Challenge – pain points

Many sustainable product SMEs in the UAE e-commerce sector encounter CRM-related inefficiencies. While early-stage practices may work on a smaller scale, they often become barriers to growth and customer engagement as businesses expand.
Among the main difficulties are:

- **Manual Communication Workflows:** Customer interactions such as post-purchase follow-ups and feedback collection are frequently handled manually across multiple messaging platforms, an approach that is inefficient and unscalable (Marie, 2024).
- **Data Sources:** Customer information is often dispersed across unintegrated systems, including email marketing software, e-commerce tools, and feedback forms, making it difficult to construct a complete view of the customer journey (Mangal & Kumar, 2025; Muhammed, 2025).
- **Absence of Real-Time Insights:** Many SMEs still rely on spreadsheets and manual data exports. Without dashboards or

advanced analytics, decisions tend to be reactive rather than proactive (Gonçalves et al., 2023; SunbaseData, 2025).

- **Underutilized Loyalty Programs:** Referral and loyalty schemes often lack personalization, making rewards predictable and reducing customer engagement. Research shows that UAE and MEA consumers increasingly prefer digital-first, personalized loyalty programs that align with their preferences (Comarch, 2025; Salesforce, 2024).

These recurring challenges highlight the need for unified CRM ecosystems powered by business intelligence. Integrated solutions that bring together communication, automation, loyalty systems, and real-time analytics can help SMEs scale responsibly, improve customer retention, and make informed decisions.

4. Proposed Solution Overview

To address the challenges of customer engagement and scattered data, the proposed solution introduces a unified CRM system designed for SMEs in the sustainable sector. The main goal is to bring all communication, customer records, and analytics into one platform so such a business can scale more easily and work more efficiently.

The system proposes to connect customer interactions across email, WhatsApp, loyalty programs, and e-commerce platforms into a single hub. This will ensure that all data is accurate, up to date, and accessible in real time. CRM also supports behavior-based automation, such as sending follow-ups after purchase or reminders for abandoned carts. This proposes to make communication more consistent and reduces the need for manual effort.

In addition, the proposed solution includes a loyalty program that will be integrated directly with the CRM. Customers can earn and redeem points in real time, which will encourage repeat purchases and build stronger brand relationships. Visual dashboards will provide clear insights into customer activity, helping the business adjust its strategy on accurate and timely data.

The proposed system is designed to be cost-effective, easy to use, and scalable, which is especially important for SMEs that are growing quickly. By aligning technology with business needs, this solution supports efficiency, customer satisfaction, and sustainable growth.

5. Technologies Involved

The intended CRM strategy of the company employs a strong suite of well-integrated digital solutions to enable data-driven decisions, personalize customer interactions, and automate processes:

- HubSpot CRM – enables behavior-based segmentation, process flows are automated, customer information is collated in one place, and personalized communications are made available across channels.
- WhatsApp Business API (via Twilio or Zoko) – Through enabling scalable, automated, and targeted messaging post-purchase, the WhatsApp Business API (via Twilio or Zoko) enables optimum customer engagement and relationship value.
- Klaviyo – By enabling dynamic customer segmentation via behavior, i.e., cart abandonment and loyalty, Klaviyo enables intelligent email marketing. It syncs with CRM data to maintain consistency in messaging.
- Smile.io – Real-time monitoring of points and rewards is possible through the gamified loyalty and referral program of Smile.io, which is linked to Shopify store and custom store of the brand.
- Microsoft Power BI – Microsoft Power BI aggregates information from all of Klaviyo, Shopify, HubSpot, and Smile.io as an attempt at creating real-time, interactive dashboards yielding actionable, meaningful business insights.
- Shopify – All-around integration on all CRM platforms, Shopify is the source e-commerce platform where master transactions and customer interactions take place.
- APIs and Webhooks – APIs and Webhooks are utilized for real-time synchronizing of customer information, loyalty reminders, and campaign statistics between sites.

6. System Diagram

The system architecture in Figure 1 illustrates how multiple digital platforms may integrate to create an interconnected, data-driven customer experience. At the entry point, Shopify and the business's e-commerce website capture customer activity, including browsing patterns, orders, referrals, and cart interactions. This data is then transmitted to other platforms in the ecosystem. HubSpot functions as the central hub, consolidating customer profiles, order histories, and engagement data while managing campaigns, loyalty programs, and WhatsApp messaging. Klaviyo supports this by enabling automated email and SMS campaigns that are triggered by specific customer behaviors, such as cart abandonment or loyalty milestone achievements. Smile.io complements these functions by

100

tracking loyalty points and referrals, feeding updated information back into both HubSpot and Klaviyo to strengthen personalization and engagement strategies. Finally, Power BI aggregates and visualizes data drawn from HubSpot, delivering interactive dashboards that support real-time monitoring, fact-based decision-making, and deeper insights into customer relationships. Together, these technologies form a cohesive ecosystem that enables SMEs to scale effectively while maintaining personalized and sustainable engagement with their customers.

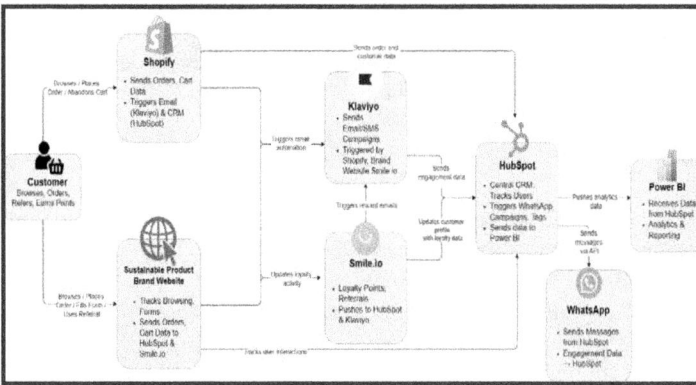

Figure 1: System architecture of the proposed CRM ecosystem integrating e-commerce, marketing automation, loyalty, and analytics platforms

7. Data Use and Analytics

Using a unified CRM system will elevate how the business captures, informs, and leverages data throughout its customer touchpoints. Previously isolated customer relations got associated with one another through the unified database, which enhances the business's 360-degree view of each customer's journey.

Using Power BI integration, live dashboards will provide visual indicators of its performance for:

- Cart abandonment trends
- Loyalty point redemption behaviors
- Click through and open rates from email or WhatsApp campaigns
- Customer segmentation by location, behaviors, or purchase patterns

It is worth highlighting that well-gathered and curated data, centralized from multiple sources, is a catalyst in improving how companies run their operations. This unified view enables teams to monitor and adjust their

101

marketing efforts in real time rather than relying on delayed manual exports. Research indicates that real-time analytics can lead to a 25% improvement in campaign ROI and help reduce customer churn through faster interventions (Wixom & Watson, 2010).

Additionally, Klaviyo's behavioral data (for example, when users abandon carts or redeem reward tiers) is synced with HubSpot, so messages can be relevant and timely. This data can be used to identify at-risk customers and forecast customer lifetime value (CLV).

Combining automation and smarter analytics shifts the system's capabilities from a purely reporting mechanism to a more proactive decision-making ecosystem, putting the business in a better position to influence its strategy with confidence.

8. Benefits

The combined CRM environment will most likely bring the following significant advantages to the sustainable product firm:

- **Better Operating Efficiency**
  Customer segmentation, customer loyalty, and automated workflow messaging significantly minimize manual communication work, liberating staff time for strategic activities.

- **Improved Customer Experience**
  Timely, personalized communication through email and WhatsApp elevates brand credibility and enhances post-purchase satisfaction.

- **Improved Customer Retention & Loyalty**
  A gamified rewards program encourages repeat purchases and referrals, increasing customer lifetime value and brand loyalty.

- **Greater Visibility of Data**
  One dashboard built in Power BI enables leadership to monitor sales, campaign, and customer activity in real time, allowing quicker and data-driven decisions.

- **Greater ROI from Marketing**
  Dynamic segmentation and behavior-based targeting reduces marketing waste and improves campaign effectiveness.

- **Scalability**
  With automated and centralized processes in place, the business can enjoy scaling customer touchpoints and operations without sacrificing on quality or customization.

9. Risks and Considerations

While the potential benefits of a CRM transformation come with considerable advantages, there are also risks and weaknesses that should always be recognized and considered to ensure realistic engagement:

1. System Integration Risks: APIs and web-hook connections between systems (HubSpot) and other solutions (e.g., Shopify) need to be monitored. Disruption can corrupt the integrity of linked data, lead to messaging errors, or affect loyalty point synchronization. Poor integration testing can cause a functional breakdown of operational processes within the business.
2. Fallback and Redundancy Measures: During integration failure, it is essential for SMEs to maintain fallback mechanisms to avoid business disruption. For example, designating Shopify as the authoritative system of record for transactional data guarantees that order history and sales records are safe even when HubSpot or Klaviyo are temporarily disconnected. Data backup, export capabilities, and clearly defined manual reconciliation processes can also provide added safeguarding. These redundancy measures ensure that critical business functions such as order processing and customer services continue without disruption while technical teams resolve integration issues.
3. Data Privacy & Compliance: When customer data is collected on one platform, maintaining GDPR-like compliance (even in non-EU markets) is crucial. Processing data in one place must keep a record of consent and a secure chain of protocols should be followed so that it ensures data cannot be misused. A few SMEs recently revealed that business owners and employees had little or no prior operational experience with handling consent and data security protocols. In several cases, breaches occurred due to poor consent practices during periods of rapid business growth (Client Services Manager, 2025).
4. Cost Escalation Over Time: Many tools used (like HubSpot) are priced on usage, and while they may not appear costly at the initial deployment, rising data volumes, message counts, or user logins can significantly increase expenses over time if not carefully monitored.
5. User Adoption Resistance: Without effective onboarding and training initiatives, users may be inhibited using features and functions or revert to old manual processes. A successful CRM transformation mostly rests not solely on the tools used, but how well those tools have been embraced into the regular everyday routines.

10. Evaluation Criteria

Several key performance indicators can be identified to assess the success of the proposed CRM system. They are rooted in improvements in customer retention, communication efficiency, marketing performance and internal adaptation.

- Customer Retention: Repeat purchase rate will serve as the primary measure, with a target of a 20% increase within the first six months of implementation.
- Communication Efficiency: Manual response times will be compared against automated CRM response times, aiming for at least a 50% reduction in manual engagement.
- Loyalty and Engagement: At least 30% of active customers are expected to participate in the loyalty and referral program. The program is designed to be frictionless and rewarding, strengthening satisfaction and advocacy.
- Marketing Performance: Segmented campaigns delivered via email and WhatsApp are projected to achieve a 25% improvement in open and click-through rates compared to previous averages.
- System Reliability: Data synchronization accuracy across HubSpot, Shopify, Klaviyo, and Smile.io will be monitored, with a target of 98% consistency. A churn prevention indicator will track the reactivation of at-risk customers, with a goal of reaching a 10% reactivation rate.
- Internal Adoption: Successful implementation will also be evaluated internally. Within two months of launch, at least 85% of relevant staff should be actively and consistently using CRM tools and dashboards.

These proposed benchmarks provide measurable targets to assess whether the system delivers on its promise of improving efficiency, customer satisfaction, and long-term sustainability.

11. Sustainability Alignment

The proposed CRM solution supports the company's sustainability goals by enhancing customer engagement and reducing resource use. Through automating communication and minimizing manual effort, the company can decrease its dependence on paperwork, various tools, and repetitive activities.

The system has a dual impact: it automates operational tasks while encouraging environmentally friendly consumer habits through customized communication. While there will be moderate upfront costs for licensing, integration, and training, the solution is naturally sustainable in the long term, as automation reduces ongoing resource waste and improves operational efficiency. Eventually, this digital strategy not only optimizes operations but also further promotes the brand's commitment to sustainability approaches.

12. Acknowledgement

We would like to acknowledge the use of generative AI tools to refine the language, phrasing, and grammar of this chapter. All ideas, structures, and content are original and authored by the contributors.

13. References

Access Partnership. (2022). *Impact of hyperscale cloud on the UAE's SMEs and start-ups.* https://accesspartnership.com/wp-content/uploads/2022/12/impact-of-hyperscale-cloud-on-the-uaes-smes-and-start-ups.pdf

BridgeRev. (2024, October 1). *How HubSpot centralizes data, making alignment between departments easier.* BridgeRev. https://www.bridgerev.com/blog/hubspot-revops-alignment

Client Services Manager. (2025, June 18). *How to Ensure Data Security and Privacy for Customer Information in CRM.* How to Ensure Data Security and Privacy for Customer Information in CRM - Client Services Manager

Comarch. (2025, February 6). *The future of customer loyalty in the MEA region: Trends, challenges, and opportunities.* Comarch. https://www.comarch.com/trade-and-services/loyalty-marketing/blog/the-future-of-customer-loyalty-in-the-mea-region-trends-challenges-and-opportunities/

Gonçalves, C. T., Gonçalves, M. J. A., & Campante, M. I. (2023). Developing Integrated Performance Dashboards Visualisations Using Power BI as a Platform. *Information, 14*(11), 614. https://doi.org/10.3390/info14110614

Hanaysha, J. R., Al-Shaikh, M. E., & Kumar, P. (2022). An Examination of Customer Relationship Management and Business Sustainability in Small and Medium Enterprises. *International Journal of Customer Relationship Marketing and Management (IJCRMM), 13*(1), 1-20. https://doi.org/10.4018/IJCRMM.300832

Nguyen, T. (2025, February 20). *Gamified loyalty program: Turning rewards into fun experiences.* Joy | Rewards & Loyalty Program for Shopify Business. https://joy.so/gamified-loyalty-program/

Klaviyo. (n.d.). *What is dynamic segmentation?* https://www.klaviyo.com/glossary/what-is-dynamic-segmentation

Kumar, V., Aksoy, L., Donkers, B., Venkatesan, R., Wiesel, T., & Tillmanns, S. (2010). Undervalued or overvalued customers: Capturing total customer engagement value. *Journal of Service*

Research, *13*(3), 297–310.
https://doi.org/10.1177/1094670510375602

Mangal, P., & Kumar, R. (2025). Use of CRM in small and medium enterprises. *International Journal of Research Publication and Reviews, 6*(4), 3616–3619. https://ijrpr.com/uploads/V6ISSUE4/IJRPR41863.pdf?utm_source=chatgpt.com

Marie, A. (2024, December 5). *Automation of customer service for your business in the UAE*. SleekFlow. https://sleekflow.io/blog/customer-service-automation-uae

Muhammed, F. (2025). *Why every SME in the Gulf needs a CRM data strategy*. LinkedIn. https://www.linkedin.com/pulse/why-every-sme-gulf-needs-crm-data-strategybefore-its-too-muhammed-oc7cc

Morshed, A. (2024). *Evaluating the influence of advanced analytics on client management systems in UAE telecom firms. Innovative Marketing , 20*(4), 41-51. doi:10.21511/im.20(4).2024.04

Outfunnel. (2025, April 15). *Seamless HubSpot and Klaviyo integration*. https://outfunnel.com/hubspot-klaviyo-integration/

Religia, Y., Ramawati, Y., Firdausi, A. S. M., and Nainggolan, D. S. (2025). Exploring digital leadership: TOE framework in CRM adoption by SMEs in developing countries. *RAUSP Management Journal, 60*(1), 52–68. Emerald Group Publishing Limited. https://doi.org/10.1108/RAUSP-06-2023-0058

Salesforce. (2024, March 8). *How companies in the UAE are winning customer loyalty*. Salesforce. https://www.salesforce.com/eu/blog/how-companies-in-uae-win-customer-loyalty/

Smile.io. (n.d.). *Smile API overview*. https://help.smile.io/en/articles/4036313-smile-api-overview

SunbaseData. (2025, March 4). *How smart dashboards reduce FTE costs & improve decision making*. SunbaseData. https://www.sunbasedata.com/blog/how-smart-dashboards-reduce-fte-costs-improve-decision-making

Twilio. (n.d.). *WhatsApp Business API*. https://www.twilio.com/en-us/messaging/channels/whatsapp

Wixom, B. H., and Watson, H. J. (2010). The BI-based organization. *International Journal of Business Intelligence Research, 1*(1), 13–28. https://doi.org/10.4018/jbir.2010071702

Zoko Team. (2025, January 29). *WhatsApp API vs Twilio: Crucial differences you must know*. https://www.zoko.io/post/whatsapp-business-api-vs-twilio

SECTION IV
SYNTHESIS

Chapter 6

Connecting the Dots: Innovation, Entrepreneurship, and the Sustainable Future

Marouane Khallouk

Abstract

This synthesis chapter connects the insights from five student-authored SME case studies to the broader fields of innovation, entrepreneurship, and sustainable business growth. Situating the cases within the UAE's Vision 2031 and Digital Economy Strategy, it highlights how operational and market fragmentation act as barriers to SME development, and how smart information systems provide entry points for overcoming them. By interpreting the student cases through established frameworks on dynamic capabilities, customer-centric value creation, and sustainable business model innovation, the chapter demonstrates how SMEs can leverage digital tools to future-proof their operations. As an academic reflection, it bridges experiential student work with entrepreneurial scholarship, offering lessons and practical pathways that align grassroots innovation with national ambitions for diversification, digitalization, and sustainability.

Keywords

Innovation; Entrepreneurship; SMEs; Digital Transformation; Sustainable Growth

---

Marouane Khallouk ✉
University of Wollongong in Dubai
MarouaneKhallouk@uowdubai.ac.ae

Khallouk, M (2025). Connecting the Dots: Innovation, Entrepreneurship, and the Sustainable Future. In Z. R. Khan, P. Bhagwat, P. Mukala, & N. Ruxwana (Eds.), *Technology adoption playbook for sustainability-focused startups and SMEs* (pp. 111-122). ENAI WG Centre for Academic Integrity in the UAE; University of Wollongong in Dubai; Gulf Book Services LTD, UK.

1. Opportunities and challenges in the UAE SME Ecosystem

1.1. SMEs at the core of UAE's growth strategy

Small and medium-sized enterprises (SMEs) sit at the centre of the UAE's national development agenda. Under "We the UAE 2031," the country targets a doubling of GDP to AED 3 trillion and AED 800 billion in non-oil exports, with a clear emphasis on building a digitally enabled economy that rewards entrepreneurial scale-ups (UAE Government, 2024).

The UAE's Digital Economy Strategy complements this by aiming to double the digital economy's GDP contribution within ten years (UAE Government, 2023; UAE Artificial Intelligence Office, n.d.). Both policies translate into concrete opportunities for SMEs, especially those that can harness smart information systems (IS) to overcome fragmentation in markets and operations.

In this context, fragmentation describes the dispersal of key activities, data, and stakeholders across disconnected systems or processes. It creates inefficiencies, slows decision-making, and limits opportunities for integration. Examining how SMEs encounter and respond to fragmentation offers a valuable lens for analysing their growth challenges.

The *Fashion SME* chapter illustrates internal operational fragmentation common to early-stage, sustainability-oriented retailers. Reliance on manual spreadsheets across sales, inventory, and reporting reduces responsiveness, increases the risk of stockouts or overstocks, and obscures impact metrics (Shaikh et al. 2025).

In contrast, the *Eco-Fashion Marketplace* highlights fragmentation on the market side. Managing a multi-vendor ecosystem of more than hundred partners, such SMEs experience order delays of two to four days and low conversion rates despite strong traffic (Hussain et al. 2025)

These two cases reveal distinct fragmentation profiles: internal inefficiencies in operations versus external coordination challenges in vendor networks. Together, they reflect two pathways for SME growth in the UAE: operations-first, which focuses on streamlining internal value activities, and platform-first, which emphasizes orchestrating external value networks. Both align closely with Vision 2031's goals of economic diversification and digitalization.

Public–private collaborations further amplify these pathways. The Dubai Department of Economy and Tourism has partnered with Noon to help SMEs expand their digital presence and reach customers more effectively (DET–Noon, 2024). This initiative lowers barriers to entry by giving smaller businesses access to established e-commerce infrastructure and logistics. Meanwhile, Emirates NBD has revamped its "Liv" digital bank, expanding mobile-first, self-service finance that provides an essential foundation for SME growth in a digital economy (Emirates NBD, 2023). These developments show how policy frameworks and corporate initiatives create an enabling environment. However, despite this progress, many SMEs continue to face persistent challenges in execution.

1.2. Entrepreneurial pain points in the UAE Context

Across both customer-facing and operations-heavy contexts, several recurring pain points are evident: scattered data, slow response times, sustainability blind spots, and weak process discipline.

In the *Next-Gen CRM* chapter, customer information is fragmented across spreadsheets, inboxes, and social channels, leaving teams without a single source of truth and forcing them to spend significant time piecing together context (Noronha et al., 2025).

The *Unified CRM Ecosystem* chapter addresses this gap through an orchestrated, multi-layered platform that integrates WhatsApp, email, loyalty programs, and e-commerce into one behaviour-driven system, supported by clear metrics for adoption and retention (Ranjbar et al., 2025).

On the operations side, both the *Fashion SME* and the *Intelligent and Sustainable Supply Chain* chapters diagnose limited real-time visibility, weak forecasting, and inconsistent sustainability reporting. Their proposed solutions include IoT tracking, AI-enabled forecasting, and Power BI dashboards, all designed to close the loop between demand planning and sustainability outcomes (Shaikh et al., 2025; Tauro et al., 2025).
These pain points are not uniquely Emirati, but the UAE context magnifies them: mobile-first consumers, fast logistics expectations, and ambitious sustainability commitments raise the bar for responsiveness and transparency.

Recent research on digital transformation shows that fragmented customer journeys and disconnected back-end systems reduce both engagement and productivity. Firms that align digital investments with well-orchestrated customer journeys and strong operational capabilities consistently outperform their peers. (Kraus et al., 2022; Lundin & Kindström., 2023; Siebert et al., 2020).

These recurring pain points highlight the gap between the UAE's enabling environment and the everyday realities faced by SMEs. While policies and corporate initiatives create opportunities, firms still struggle to translate them into practice. The next section explores how entrepreneurship,

111

supported by smart information systems, can turn these challenges into pathways for value creation.

1.3. The role of entrepreneurship and smart IS

Entrepreneurial teams across the five chapters demonstrate how smart information systems can generate new sources of value. The *Fashion Marketplace* chapter embeds analytics, automation, and sustainability tracking as central capabilities rather than peripheral ones (Hussain et al., 2025). The *Fashion SME* chapter similarly integrates business intelligence tools to align operations with sustainable growth (Shaikh et al., 2025). *Intelligent and Sustainable Supply Chain* chapter develops an intelligent and sustainability-aware supply chain by combining IoT, AI, and integrated dashboards (Tauro et al., 2025). The CRM chapters, *Next-Gen* and *Unified*, re-engineer customer engagement through unified data, workflow automation, and omnichannel orchestration (Noronha et al., 2025; Ranjbar et al., 2025).

This pattern reflects recent research on dynamic capabilities, which argues that firms gain advantage not merely from owning assets but from their ability to sense opportunities, seize them, and transform processes through digital capabilities that continuously reconfigure data and operations (Rahman et al., 2025; Al-Moaid & Almarhdi., 2024). The trajectory of Careem illustrates this logic in the UAE context. By evolving from a ride-hailing service into a regional "everything app" and attracting a $400 million investment from e&, Careem scaled into payments, groceries, and logistics through a platform and data-first architecture (Reuters, 2023; Careem, 2025).

Taken together, these cases and examples show that entrepreneurship and smart IS act as twin engines of value creation.

2. Business & management models to create value.

2.1. Customer-centric value creation

A comparison of the *Next-Gen CRM*, *Unified CRM*, and *Eco-Fashion Marketplace* chapters reveals a common theme: unified data combined with journey-oriented orchestration drives stronger engagement and higher conversion.

Contemporary CRM research has moved beyond viewing CRM as a simple tool. It now emphasizes integration across the entire customer journey, robust data governance, and AI-enabled decision-making. Recent reviews highlight the rise of "social CRM" and analytics-driven approaches that directly link to business performance (Perez-Vega et al., 2022; Guerola-Navarro et al., 2024).

In these cases, RAP-style plugins and ecosystem orchestration bring all customer interactions into a single context, enabling faster responses, paperless onboarding, and predictive prioritization. The *Unified CRM* chapter's design builds on this foundation by adding loyalty mechanisms and WhatsApp integration to strengthen lifecycle value.

Recent service research replaces a narrow focus on service-quality measures with an emphasis on AI-enabled experience design and omnichannel coherence. Huang and Rust (2021) provide a strategic framework for identifying where and how AI enhances the service process to improve engagement and outcomes. In parallel, B2B and platform scholars show how digitized journeys and access-based models are reshaping customer touchpoints, expectations, and metrics (Lundin & Kindström, 2023; Trujillo-Torres et al., 2024).

The UAE provides concrete examples of these dynamics. Noon's partnership with the Dubai Department of Economy and Tourism illustrates how platform orchestration reduces seller friction and expands digital access for SMEs (DET–Noon, 2024). Emirates NBD's revamp of its Liv digital bank demonstrates how customer experience can be rapidly adapted to the expectations of "Gen Now" consumers (Emirates NBD, 2023).

2.2. Operational excellence and resource efficiency

The *Fashion SME*, *Supply Chain*, and the *Fashion Marketplace* chapters converge on a second thesis: lean flow combined with digital visibility creates both resilience and efficiency. Recent studies integrate lean management with Industry 4.0, showing how sensors, analytics, and automation reduce the eight classical wastes and support cultures of continuous problem solving (Cifone et al., 2021; Schumacher et al., 2023; Galeazzo et al., 2024).

In these cases, IoT-enabled inventory, AI-driven forecasting, and integrated dashboards provide earlier signals and faster decision cycles (Shaikh et al., 2025; Tauro et al., 2025; Hussain et al., 2025). The *Fashion Marketplace* further improves efficiency through its vendor engine, which streamlines onboarding and communication to shorten multi-day delays (Hussain et al., 2025).

Examples from the UAE reinforce these insights. Majid Al Futtaim has invested heavily in data-driven retail logistics and omnichannel integration, coinciding with a 15 percent rise in e-commerce spending in 2023 (MAF, 2024). The Dubai Roads and Transport Authority has expanded its Intelligent Traffic Systems across main roads, demonstrating how real-time operations, automation, and analytics can be scaled citywide (Dubai RTA, 2024; 2025).

Supply chain research after 2020 also highlights the connection between sustainability, resilience, and viability. Sustainable supply chain management (SSCM) practices strengthen robustness and recovery while enhancing overall performance (Eggert & Hartmann, 2022; Pan et al., 2025). This perspective aligns closely with *Supply Chain* chapter's sustainability tracker and the *Fashion Marketplace* chapter's impact engine, both of which close the loop from demand to measurable environmental outcomes (Tauro et al., 2025; Hussain et al., 2025).

2.3. Sustainability as competitive advantage

The current conversation on sustainability extends well beyond regulatory compliance. Recent studies on sustainable business model innovation (SBMI) and shared value show that firms gain a competitive edge when they embed social and environmental objectives into their value proposition, their processes of value creation, and their mechanisms of value capture (Mignon & Bankel, 2023; Geissdoerfer et al., 2018).
Research on the Triple Bottom Line (TBL) also emphasizes the importance of rigorous measurement and integration, warning against rhetorical commitments that are not supported by concrete action (Yip et al., 2023)

In the five student chapters, sustainability is operationalized in practice. The *Fashion SME* and *Supply Chain* Chapters quantify waste reduction and carbon savings through dashboards (Shaikh et al., 2025; Tauro et al., 2025). The *Fashion Marketplace* communicates sustainability through customer-facing impact narratives (Hussain et al., 2025). The CRM chapters contribute by reducing paper use, rework, and repeat queries through automation (Noronha et al., 2025; Ranjbar et al., 2025).

Evidence from the UAE further demonstrates how these lessons take shape in practice. Masdar City illustrates how place-based ecosystems make sustainability visible, measurable, and investable through its reporting frameworks and ongoing programs (Masdar City, 2025).

3. Practical recommendations for UAE SMEs

3.1. Cross-case lessons for entrepreneurs

Three cross-case lessons stand out:
- **Integrate before you innovate.**

Each case's breakthrough begins with integration. RAP plugins unify channels, CRM ecosystems centralize data, and IoT with AI brings supply and demand signals together. Integration serves as the foundation for analytics, automation, and sustainability reporting

- **Build dynamic capabilities, not single tools**

The most resilient SMEs build three interrelated capabilities. They strengthen sensing through dashboards and analytics, seizing through automations and workflows, and transforming through iterative roadmaps. Recent research shows that these digital dynamic capabilities are central to successful transformation in SMEs, particularly in emerging-market contexts (Rahman et al., 2025; Al-Moaid et al., 2024).

- **Make sustainability quantifiable and communicable.**

Moving from claims to measurable metrics creates both differentiation and trust. This is precisely what the *Fashion Marketplace* and *Supply Chain* chapters have proposed, and it reflects what buyers increasingly expect (Eggert & Hartmann, 2023; Pan et al., 2025). These lessons highlight three possible entry points evident in the cases. A customer-first approach is illustrated by *Next-Gen CRM* and *Unified CRM*. An operations-first approach appears in the *Fashion SME* and *Supply Chain*. A sustainability-first approach is demonstrated by the *Fashion Marketplace*. Although the starting points differ, all converge on the need for integrated data foundations.

3.2. Recommendations for UAE SMEs

- **Stage 1: Diagnosis**

Map current customer journeys and internal processes and identify points of fragmentation or waste such as duplicate data entry, slow first responses, and frequent stockouts.

Conduct a lightweight audit of systems and data flows, tracing how information moves from channels through the CRM to the warehouse and business intelligence platforms.

Benchmark against UAE exemplars. The Noon and Dubai Department of Economy and Tourism partnership illustrates the value of smooth digital onboarding for sellers, while the Roads and Transport Authority's intelligent systems demonstrate the benefits of real-time operational visibility (DET–Noon, 2024; Dubai RTA, 2024).

- **Stage 2: Pilot**

Select one high-impact process and integrate it end to end. The cases illustrate this pattern in different ways:

- Customer-first pilot: Deploy a RAP plugin that connects WhatsApp with the CRM, supported by response-time automation and a micro-dashboard to monitor first-reply performance.
- Operations-first pilot: Introduce IoT inventory tags in a single warehouse and apply AI forecasting for two SKUs, with results tracked through a Power BI dashboard.
- Sustainability-first pilot: Launch a customer-facing widget that displays water and carbon savings at the point of order confirmation.

SMEs can also leverage UAE platforms and hubs to accelerate these pilots. Dubai SME provides advisory services, Hub71 in Abu Dhabi offers venture support, and the DIFC Innovation Hub enables fintech-grade data governance and regulatory technology practices.

- **Stage 3: Scale**
Extend integrations gradually across channels and functions and formalize both data governance and change management.
Add loyalty mechanisms and advanced analytics models to enhance customer engagement.

Use stage-gates that link directly to customer, efficiency, and sustainability KPIs. In practice, this means setting checkpoints that measure accuracy, net promoter scores, fulfilment speed, and environmental impact.
Financing and partnerships should also be considered. Emirates NBD's Liv platform and other digital banking tools provide SME-friendly financial infrastructure, while Noon's programs can accelerate access to digital markets (Emirates NBD, 2023; DET–Noon, 2024).

4. Future proofing through ecosystem integration

SME transformation is best understood as an ecosystem activity. The cases collectively show that scaling occurs when vendors, customers, and data partners are connected through shared standards and APIs.

In the UAE, government and corporate platforms reduce the cost of this integration. Examples include Dubai Future Accelerators, the DET–Noon programs, fintech sandboxes that enable bank-grade experimentation, and city systems such as the RTA's Intelligent Traffic Systems, which provide reliable data and benchmarks (UAE Government, 2024; DET–Noon, 2024; Dubai RTA, 2025). For sustainability, firms can look to ecosystem exemplars such as Masdar City, where sustainability reporting and smart-mobility initiatives offer templates and partnerships for pilot validation (Masdar City, 2025).

5. References

Al-Moaid, N.A.A. & Almarhdi, S.G., (2024). Developing dynamic capabilities for successful digital transformation projects: The mediating role of change management. *Journal of Innovation and Entrepreneurship*, *13*(1), p.85.

Careem (2025) *Careem's 2024 roundup*, 4 February. Available at: https://blog.careem.com/posts/careem-2024-roundup

Cifone, F.D., Hoberg, K., Holweg, M. & Staudacher, A.P., (2021). 'Lean 4.0': how can digital technologies support lean practices?. *International Journal of Production Economics*, *241*, p.108258.

Dubai Department of Economy & Tourism (DET) (2024) *DET and Noon sign pioneering e-commerce partnership*, 10 September. Available at: https://www.dubaidet.gov.ae/en/newsroom/press-releases/det-noon-e-commerce-partnership

Dubai Roads and Transport Authority (RTA) (2024) *RTA launches Phase II study of Intelligent Traffic Systems initiative*, 23 June. Available at: https://www.mediaoffice.ae/en/news/2024/june/23-06/rta-launches-phase-ii-study-of-intelligent-traffic-systems-initiative

Dubai Roads and Transport Authority (RTA) (2025) *Organising the Artificial Intelligence Exhibition 2025 Featuring a Platform for 11 Initiatives*, 7 July. Available at: https://www.rta.ae/wps/portal/rta/ae/home/news-and-media/all-news/NewsDetails/organising-the-artificial-intelligence-exhibition-2025-featuring-a-platform-for-11-initiatives

Eggert, J. & Hartmann, J., 2023. Sustainable supply chain management—a key to resilience in the global pandemic. *Supply Chain Management: An International Journal*, *28*(3), pp.486-507.

Emirates NBD (2023) *Emirates NBD revamps digital bank Liv with new value proposition targeting Gen Now*, 13 July. Available at: https://www.emiratesnbd.com/en/media-center/emirates-nbd-revamps-digital-bank-liv-with-new-value-proposition-targeting-gen-now

Galeazzo, A., Furlan, A., Tosetto, D. & Vinelli, A., 2024. Are lean and digital engaging better problem solvers? An empirical study on Italian manufacturing firms. *International Journal of Operations & Production Management*, *44*(6), pp.1217-1248.

Geissdoerfer, M., Vladimirova, D. & Evans, S. (2018) 'Sustainable business model innovation: A review', *Journal of Cleaner Production*, 198, pp.401–416.

Guerola-Navarro, V., Gil-Gomez, H., Oltra-Badenes, R. & Soto-Acosta, P., (2024). Customer relationship management and its impact on entrepreneurial marketing: A literature review. *International Entrepreneurship and Management Journal*, *20*(2), pp.507-547.

Huang, M.H. & Rust, R.T., (2021). Engaged to a robot? The role of AI in service. *Journal of Service Research*, *24*(1), pp.30-41.

Hussain, T. S., Kumar, A. A., & Elgamil, M. (2025). Building a Conscious Commerce Engine: A Smart IS Framework for a UAE-based eco-friendly fashion marketplace. In Z. R. Khan, P. Bhagwat, P. Mukala, & N. Ruxwana (Eds.), *Technology adoption playbook for sustainability-focused startups and SMEs* (pp. 61-77). ENAI WG Centre for Academic Integrity in the UAE; University of Wollongong in Dubai; Gulf Book Services LTD, UK.

Kraus, S., Durst, S., Ferreira, J.J., Veiga, P., Kailer, N. & Weinmann, A., (2022). Digital transformation in business and management research: An overview of the current status quo. *International journal of information management*, *63*, 102466.

Lundin, L. & Kindström, D., 2023. Digitalizing customer journeys in B2B markets. *Journal of Business Research*, *157*, p.113639.

Majid Al Futtaim (2024) *State of the UAE Retail Economy 2023*, 4 April. Available at: https://www.majidalfuttaim.com/en/media-centre/press-releases/detail/2024/04/majid-al-futtaim-s-state-of-the-uae-retail-economy-report-reveals-double-digit-consumer-spending-increase-in-2023

Masdar City (2025) *Sustainability reports; WFES 2025 highlights*. Available at: https://masdarcity.ae/sustainable-urban-development/sustainability-reports

Mignon, I. & Bankel, A., (2023). Sustainable business models and innovation strategies to realize them: A review of 87 empirical cases. *Business Strategy and the Environment*, *32*(4), pp.1357-1372.

Noronha, N., Dypiangco, R.., D'souza, F., & Mathew, N (2025). Next-Gen CRMs for SMEs: Enhancing Customer Engagement with RAP Plugins. In Z. R. Khan, P. Bhagwat, P. Mukala, & N. Ruxwana (Eds.), *Technology adoption playbook for sustainability-focused startups and SMEs* (pp. 81-95). ENAI WG Centre for Academic Integrity in the UAE; University of Wollongong in Dubai; Gulf Book Services LTD, UK.

Pan, S., Ivanov, D., Chutani, A., Xing, X., Jia, F.J. & Huang, G.Q., (2025). New normal, new norms: Towards sustainable and resilient global logistics and supply chain management. *Transportation Research Part E: Logistics and Transportation Review*, *201*, p.104276.

Perez-Vega, R., Hopkinson, P., Singhal, A. & Mariani, M.M., (2022). From CRM to social CRM: A bibliometric review and research agenda for consumer research. *Journal of Business Research*, *151*, pp.1-16.

Rahman, S.A., Taghizadeh, N.S., Tipu, S.A.A. & Far, S.M., (2025). Leveraging dynamic capabilities for digital transformation: Exploring the moderating role of cost in environmental performance of SMEs. *Journal of Open Innovation: Technology, Market, and Complexity*, *11*(2), p.100523.

Ranjbar, S., Islam, F., & Virani, H. (2025). Enabling Business Intelligence through Unified CRM Ecosystems. In Z. R. Khan, P. Bhagwat, P. Mukala, & N. Ruxwana (Eds.), *Technology adoption playbook for sustainability-focused startups and SMEs* (pp. 97-108). ENAI WG Centre for Academic Integrity in the UAE; University of Wollongong in Dubai; Gulf Book Services LTD, UK

Reuters (2023) *UAE's e& takes $400 million majority stake in Careem's super app*, 10 April. Available at: https://www.reuters.com/markets/deals/uaes-e-takes-400-mln-majority-stake-ride-hailer-careems-super-app-2023-04-10/

Schumacher, S., Hall, R., Bildstein, A. & Bauernhansl, T., (2023). Lean Production Systems 4.0: systematic literature review and field study on the digital transformation of lean methods and tools. *International Journal of Production Research*, *61*(24), pp.8751-8773.

Shaikh, A. N., Sujith, A., Bikram, R. S., & Roy, A. (2025). Empowering Sustainable Growth with Smart IS – The Fashion SME. In Z. R. Khan, P. Bhagwat, P. Mukala, & N. Ruxwana (Eds.), *Technology adoption playbook for sustainability-focused startups and SMEs* (pp. 27–40). ENAI WG Centre for Academic Integrity in the UAE; University of Wollongong in Dubai; Gulf Book Services LTD, UK

Siebert, A., Gopaldas, A. & Simões, C. (2020) 'Customer experience journeys: Loyalty loops vs. involvement spirals', *Journal of Marketing*, 84(4), pp.45-66.

Tauro, A. N., Varughese, A., Sapavat, A. S. & Arar, L. (2025). Intelligent & Sustainable Supply Chain for Smart Retail. In Z. R. Khan, P. Bhagwat, P. Mukala, & N. Ruxwana (Eds.), *Technology adoption playbook for sustainability-focused startups and SMEs* (pp. 43-58). ENAI WG Centre for Academic Integrity in the UAE; University of Wollongong in Dubai; Gulf Book Services LTD, UK.

Trujillo-Torres, L., Anlamlier, E., Mimoun, L., Chatterjee, L. & Dion, D., (2024). Access-based customer journeys. *Journal of the Academy of Marketing Science*, *52*(1), pp.24-43.

UAE Artificial Intelligence, Digital Economy & Remote Work Applications Office (n.d.) *Digital economy*. Available at: https://ai.gov.ae/digital-economy/

UAE Government (2023) *Digital Economy Strategy*, 5 September. Available at: https://u.ae/en/about-the-uae/strategies-initiatives-and-awards/strategies-plans-and-visions/finance-and-economy/digital-economy-strategy

UAE Government (2024) *We the UAE 2031' vision*, 22 April. Available at: https://u.ae/en/about-the-uae/strategies-initiatives-and-awards/strategies-plans-and-visions/innovation-and-future-shaping/we-the-uae-2031-vision

Yip, W.S., Zhou, H. & To, S., (2023). A critical analysis on the triple bottom line of sustainable manufacturing: key findings and implications. *Environmental Science and Pollution Research*, 30(14), pp.41388-41404.

Advancing Smart IS Adoption for UAE SMEs: Conclusion, Reflections, and Recommendations

Patrick Mukala . Nkqubela Ruxwana . Zeenath Reza Khan . Pradnya Bhagwat

Abstract

This chapter concludes the Technology Adoption Playbook for Sustainability-Focused Startups and SMEs, highlighting how Smart Information Systems (Smart IS) enable UAE SMEs to achieve sustainable digital transformation. It outlines three guiding principles for future readiness. First, integration precedes innovation, so SMEs must build cohesive systems before scaling technologies. Second, sustainability must be measurable, with clear environmental and social metrics embedded in digital strategies. Third, ecosystem partnerships accelerate growth by fostering collaboration among academia, industry, and government. Drawing on student-authored cases, the chapter illustrates how AI, automation, cloud computing, and data analytics strengthen competitiveness, resilience, and ethical governance. Aligned with the UAE Digital Government Strategy 2025 and Vision 2031, it offers practical recommendations for SMEs, policymakers, and educators to drive responsible, data-driven innovation. Ultimately, Smart IS adoption is presented as a strategic pathway to inclusive, future-proofed growth and long-term economic sustainability in the UAE and beyond.

Keywords

Smart Information Systems, Digital Transformation, Sustainability, SMEs, UAE Innovation Ecosystem

---

Patrick Mukala
University of Wollongong in Dubai

Nkqubela Ruxwana
University of Wollongong in Dubai

Zeenath Reza Khan ✉
University of Wollongong in Dubai
zeenathkhan@uowdubai.ac.ae

Pradnya Bhagwat
University of Wollongong in Dubai

Mukala, P., Ruxwana, N. Khan, Z. R., & Bhagwat, P. (2025). *Advancing Smart IS Adoption for UAE SMEs: Conclusion, Reflections, and Recommendations.* In Z. R. Khan, P. Bhagwat, P. Mukala, & N. Ruxwana (Eds.), *Technology adoption playbook for sustainability-focused startups and SMEs* (pp. 123-140). ENAI WG Centre for Academic Integrity in the UAE; University of Wollongong in Dubai; Gulf Book Services LTD, UK.

1. Introduction and Contextualization

This *Playbook* concludes a collective journey that bridges classroom innovation with real-world SME transformation across the UAE's dynamic digital economy. Through each student-authored case, it has demonstrated how applied learning, responsible technology adoption, and smart information systems (Smart IS) can translate theoretical insight into measurable business impact.

As organizations navigate an era of rapid technological acceleration, the challenge is no longer whether to transform but how to sustain competitiveness amid constant change. Companies with mature digital and AI capabilities consistently deliver greater value creation over time, while those slow to adapt risk obsolescence (McKinsey, 2024; Franzè et al., 2024). Digital transformation has thus become a defining test of adaptability, sustainability, and innovation. It serves as a strategic bridge between technological potential and organizational execution, integrating governance, data, and capability-building frameworks to deliver measurable improvements in performance and innovation (Yang et al., 2025; Wei & Shen, 2025).

Across the *Playbook*, technologies such as AI, Power BI, automation, big data analytics, and cloud computing have been shown to reshape SME operations, enhance customer engagement, and drive sustainable innovation (Ali et al., 2024; Hussain et al., 2025; Noronha et al., 2025; Ranjsbar et al., 2025; Shaikh et al., 2025; Tauro et al., 2025). These cases collectively affirm that the future of SME resilience depends on how effectively organizations align technology integration with ethical, sustainable, and human-centered practices.

Small and Medium Enterprises (SMEs) play a pivotal role in the UAE's economic diversification agenda, driving innovation, employment, and sustainable growth. As demonstrated throughout this Technology Adoption *Playbook*, digital transformation is a strategic imperative for SMEs seeking to build resilient, competitive organizations capable of thriving in the Fourth Industrial Revolution. This concluding chapter synthesizes insights from all student-authored cases, highlighting the benefits of digital adoption and offering actionable recommendations for SMEs, policymakers, and academic institutions. Future-proofing SMEs requires resilience, flexibility, and foresight, enabling them to anticipate potential scenarios and disruptions (Omand, 2013; Awad & Martín-Rojas, 2024; Khan, 2025). It is a strategic approach that combines adaptable strategies, innovative mindsets, and proactive risk management to ensure long-term sustainability and competitiveness (Manu, 2021). Central to this approach is the ability to respond effectively to market shifts through financial planning, diversification, innovation, and customer-centric strategies.

Integrating Smart IS and emerging technologies such as AI, IoT, blockchain, big data, and automation is crucial for enhancing SMEs' competitiveness, operational efficiency, and adaptability. Effective adoption requires a focus on digital transformation, continuous innovation, workforce training, and data security to navigate evolving market demands and technological change. Real-world examples across sectors, including healthcare and supply chain management, illustrate how these technologies drive growth, create competitive advantage, and future-proof enterprises.

The *Playbook* is organized around four thematic pathways: *Operations-first, Market- first, Customer-first, and Synthesis*, with each reflecting a strategic approach to digital maturity:

i. **Operations-first** emphasizes internal optimization through automation, analytics, and smart systems to enhance efficiency and resilience.

ii. **Market-first** focuses on ecosystem integration and strategic use of data to strengthen market positioning.

iii. **Customer-first** highlights intelligent, data-driven engagement and predictive in- sights to enhance customer relationships.

iv. **Synthesis** integrates these pathways, underlining the importance of aligning Smart IS adoption with national digital strategies and sustainability goals to future-proof SMEs.

Together, these themes establish a consistent narrative: sustainable digital trans- formation requires integrated, human-centered, and data-driven strategies that balance operational excellence, market responsiveness, and customer-centric innovation. Critically, these strategies must recognize that integration precedes innovation, sustainability outcomes need to be measurable, and ecosystem partnerships play a pivotal role in accelerating growth and resilience.

2. Key Insights on Technology Adoption for SMEs

This *Playbook* highlights how digital transformation future-proofs organizations by integrating people, processes, and platforms. Within the UAE context, it aligns with the UAE Digital Government Strategy 2025 and AI Strategy 2031, demonstrating how Smart IS, data analytics, and cloud computing enhance efficiency, sustainability, and customer engagement (UAE Digital Government, 2023). Examples such as Power BI-driven dashboards, Azure automation, and AI analytics show how SMEs can convert data into actionable intelligence, while the *Conscious Commerce Engine* (Hussain et al., 2025) and *Sustainable Fashion SME* (Shaikh et al., 2025) chapters illustrate how modular, cloud-based architectures foster agility and sustainability (Ma & Zhu., 2023).

Building on the *Conscious Commerce Engine* described in Chapter 3, the *Playbook* demonstrates that digital transformation is most effective when it aligns commercial efficiency with ethical and sustainability objectives. Integrating AI, analytics, and transparent sustainability tracking shifts Smart IS from a transactional tool to a driver of trust-based commerce.

3. Key Cross-Cutting Lessons

The analysis and case studies presented throughout this *Playbook* highlight the critical lessons and strategic principles that SMEs in the UAE can adopt to future-proof their businesses, leveraging Smart IS and emerging technologies for growth, resilience, and sustainability, with the following key cross-cutting lessons:

3.1. Integration Precedes Innovation

Establishing cohesive systems and processes is essential before advanced technologies can drive meaningful innovation. Research indicates that SMEs benefit from integrating disruptive technologies within ecosystem-based business models to enhance digital transformation outcomes (Hafeez et al., 2025). Additionally, the development of digital transformation strategies that consider the unique characteristics of SMEs is crucial for successful implementation (Romero & Mammadov, 2025).

This principle is exemplified by the CRM transformation case studies, which highlight how integrating disparate data sources and communication channels into a centralized system is a foundational step before leveraging AI and analytics for innovation. The *Next-Gen CRMs* chapter (Noronha et al., 202) demonstrates how RAP plugins create an integrated customer-operations hub, while the *Unified CRM Ecosystem* chapter (Ranjbar et al., 2025) shows how centralizing communications across multiple platforms enables advanced analytics and automation.

The *Sustainable Fashion SME* chapter reinforces this lesson by showing how cloud-based automation and modular AI forecasting streamlined internal workflows, transforming data fragmentation into coordinated decision-making. By integrating Power BI and Azure Machine Learning, the enterprise demonstrated that internal process discipline is a prerequisite for sustainable innovation.

3.2. Sustainability Must Be Measurable

Tracking, monitoring, and reporting sustainability outcomes is crucial for credibility, compliance, and strategic impact. Studies highlight the importance of performance evaluations in digital transformation, focusing on measurable sustainability metrics to guide SMEs toward sustainable practices (Melo et al., 2023). Furthermore, integrating sustainable practices into digital transformation initiatives within SMEs can lead to improved performance and long-term viability.

The *Unified CRM Ecosystem* chapter demonstrates this by using Power BI dashboards to track sustainability metrics and customer engagement, ensuring that environmental goals are quantifiable and aligned with business operations. Both CRM cases emphasize automated document tracking and sustainability metrics to meet compliance and enhance brand credibility.

Likewise, the *Intelligent Supply Chain chapter* (Ashton et al., 2025) highlights measurable sustainability through IoT sensors and Power BI dashboards aligned with the UAE Green Agenda 2030. Real-time tracking of emissions, waste, and logistics efficiency exemplifies how digital tools can make sustainability quantifiable and visible.

3.3. Ecosystem Partnerships Accelerate Growth

Collaboration across suppliers, customers, regulators, and academic institutions enhances resources, capabilities, and market reach. Evidence suggests that SMEs can leverage partner ecosystems to achieve growth through collaboration, economies of scale, and faster digital transformation (Romero & Mammadov, 2025). Moreover, strategic partnerships within entrepreneurial ecosystems play a key role in the success of SMEs in the digitalization environment.

The *Next-Gen CRMs* chapter illustrates this using RAP

plugins and API integrations with platforms like WhatsApp Business and Instagram, showcasing how partnerships with technology providers can streamline customer engagement and operational processes. The *Unified CRM Ecosystem* chapter demonstrates integration with multiple platforms including HubSpot, Shopify, and Klaviyo, enabling seamless data flow and enhanced customer experiences.

4. Additional Strategic Insights

4.1. Adaptable Strategies are Essential

Futureproofing requires flexible approaches that embrace emerging technologies and foster a culture of continuous innovation. SMEs must adopt systems approaches to digital technology integration to build resilient innovation capabilities and maintain sustain- able growth trajectories (da Silva et al., 2025). Additionally, constructing digital transformation strategy frameworks for SMEs can generate resilience and antifragility, enabling them to navigate the complexities of the digital era (Sagala & Őri, 2024).

4.2. Digital Transformation is Crucial for Competitiveness

In a rapidly evolving technological landscape, SMEs must adopt digital transformation strategies to remain competitive. The OECD emphasizes that enabling SME digitalization is a top policy priority to overcome size-related limitations and enhance performance (OECD, 2021). Furthermore, digital transformation is a powerful driver of competitiveness in SME manufacturing, as it enhances operational efficiency and market responsiveness (da Silva et al., 2025).

4.3. Smart IS Drives Growth and Resilience

Technologies such as AI, machine learning, IoT, and data analytics are instrumental in driving growth, innovation, and resilience across industries. Studies demonstrate that digital transformation can enhance sustainable organizational performance by improving firms' sustainable innovation capabilities (Wang & Zhang, 2024). Moreover, the adoption of digital technologies and business intelligence tools facilitates data-driven decision-making, optimizing operational efficiency and profitability in SMEs (Kallmuenzer et al., 2024).

Integrated Transformation Strategies Lead to Superior Outcomes

SMEs that implement integrated digital transformation strategies achieve superior profitability and market valuation. Research indicates that SMEs integrating digital transformation and innovation within sustainable entrepreneurship frameworks can improve overall sustainability practices and competitiveness (Sudirman et al., 2025; Wang & Zhang, 2025). Additionally, enhancing digital technology adoption in SMEs through sustainable resilience strategies can positively impact their performance and adaptability (Sudirman et al., 2025).

Throughout the cases presented in this *Playbook*, it is evident that neglecting digital transformation exposes SMEs to critical risks. These include not only loss of market relevance, competitive disadvantage, rising operational costs, regulatory noncompliance, and erosion of customer trust, but also risks associated with failing to integrate systems before pursuing innovation, the inability to measure and monitor sustainability impacts, and missed opportunities from underutilized ecosystem partnerships. Ultimately, sustainable success in the digital era depends not merely on adopting technology but on embedding digital transformation as a core organizational philosophy that emphasizes integration, measurable sustainability, and strategic collaboration.

5. Benefits of Digital Transformation for SMEs

The *Playbook*'s digital transformation frameworks collectively illustrate how SMEs can leverage Smart IS to achieve multidimensional benefits through strategic technology adoption. These benefits align with global insights on digital competitiveness from McKinsey (2023), OECD (2024), and Deloitte (2024). In this context, futureproofing has become essential for organizations seeking to maintain a competitive edge and secure long-term success. Futureproofing entails proactive measures that strengthen businesses, enhance adaptability, and enable SMEs to thrive amid changing market conditions and economic uncertainty. Across the cases presented in this *Playbook*, several key benefits emerged from Smart IS adoption:

5.1. Operational and Financial Efficiency

Automation of reporting, analytics, and demand forecasting reduces manual work and error rates while improving inventory management accuracy (Amosu et al., 2024). Machine learning-driven forecasting can enhance planning accuracy by up to 50%, reducing overstock and waste

(McKinsey, 2017). Real-time dashboards using Power BI enable faster decision cycles, improving productivity and profitability (Frempong et al, 2022). In the *Sustainable Fashion SME* and Supply Chain chapters, automation of reporting and IoT-enabled monitoring improved inventory accuracy, reduced waste, and lowered costs. These examples extend the efficiency narrative beyond CRM transformation into production and logistics, showing how Smart IS optimizes both back-end and market-facing operations. The *Next-Gen CRMs* chapter demonstrates how automation and RAP plugins can save up to 11 hours weekly per employee, translating to significant cost savings and error reduction.

5.2. Strategic Agility and Innovation

Through intelligent analytics and AI, SMEs can identify market trends and emerging customer preferences, allowing them to tailor offerings dynamically. AI-enhanced customer segmentation improves engagement, while predictive tools enable proactive resource allocation and innovation (Wedel & Kamakura, 2000; Kolawole, 2023). The *Unified CRM Ecosystem* chapter (Ranjsbar et al., 2025) highlights how behavior-based segmentation and automated workflows enable personalized marketing and rapid response to customer needs.

5.3. Sustainability and ESG Integration

Technology-driven sustainability dashboards empower SMEs to quantify and communicate environmental impacts. By tracking waste reduction, emissions, and material use, enterprises align with circular economy principles (Geissdoerfer et al., 2017) and the UN Sustainable Development Goals (United Nations, 2015). Integrating sustainability KPIs within digital systems also enhances investor and consumer trust (Hristov & Chirico, 2019). Both CRM cases emphasize the importance of automated document tracking and sustainability metrics to meet compliance and enhance brand credibility.

5.4. Inclusive Growth and Social Impact

Smart IS adoption democratizes innovation for resource-constrained enterprises, allowing micro and small businesses to compete with larger corporations. Technology thus acts as an equalizer, reducing market entry barriers and fostering inclusive participation in the digital economy (Li, 2025; OECD, 2024). The *Unified CRM Ecosystem* case shows how

131

centralized, affordable CRM tools enable SMEs to scale efficiently and compete with larger players.

6. Recommendations

Building on the insights and case studies presented in this *Playbook*, the following recommendations provide guidance for SMEs, policymakers, and academic institutions to advance digital transformation and future-proof businesses:

6.1. For SMEs and Entrepreneurs

i.   adopt digital transformation incrementally, beginning with affordable, cloud-based systems that deliver measurable ROI

ii. Invest in digital literacy and staff upskilling to ensure human readiness

iii. Integrate sustainability metrics into dashboards to track and communicate environ- mental performance

iv. Leverage AI and analytics as decision-support tools rather than replacements for human judgment

v.   Prioritize cybersecurity and ethical data management to build consumer trust and ensure regulatory compliance (NIST, 2024; ISO/IEC 27001:2022)

vi. The Next-Gen CRMs case underscores the importance of phased implementation, starting with high-impact processes like customer onboarding and communication automation

6.2. For Policymakers and Reg

i.   Develop incentive schemes such as digital adoption grants and low-interest technology financing for SMEs

ii. Promote interoperable data infrastructures to facilitate SME participation in digital ecosystems

iii. Strengthen public-private partnerships for digital skilling and sustainability-driven innovation

iv. Establish regulatory sandboxes to encourage experimentation with AI, blockchain, and automation

v.   Enhance support for cybersecurity awareness and compliance readiness (NIST, 2024; ISO/IEC 27001:2022)

vi. Codify interoperable data standards and privacy-by-design requirements to enable SMEs to participate in

132

trusted digital ecosystems and leverage partnerships effectively (UAE Digital Government Strategy 2025; NIST, 2024)

6.3. For Academia and Capacity Builders

i. Embed digital transformation and sustainability in business and IT curricula to prepare future-ready graduates

ii. Foster collaboration between universities, incubators, and SMEs to codevelop digital prototypes and applied research

iii. Encourage multidisciplinary learning that connects business strategy, technology, and ethics

iv. Build on existing project-based learning models that address real-world SME challenges, as exemplified by this Playbook, while further strengthening their application to drive deeper digital transformation outcomes

v. The student-authored cases in this Playbook demonstrate the value of hands-on, interdisciplinary projects in bridging theory and practice

7. Final Reflections

In today's volatile markets and rapid technological revolution, technology adoption for businesses of all sizes globally is not merely a matter of modernization but a strategic pathway to sustainability, competitiveness, and resilience. It is especially critical for SMEs in the UAE, where rapidly evolving technologies and intense competitive pressures require adaptability, proactive strategies, and robust measures to future-proof their operations.

Across the chapters, this *Playbook* emphasizes that the foundation of business resilience and long-term sustainability lies in the strategic adoption of Smart IS and emerging technologies. By addressing the key pain points of SMEs, fragmented systems, data silos, skill gaps, and limited sustainability tracking, it demonstrates that digital transformation can be achievable, scalable, and inclusive. When technology is leveraged purposefully, SMEs can move from reactive operational models to proactive, innovation-driven enterprises capable of generating measurable value and contributing meaningfully to the UAE's sustainable economic growth.

As highlighted in Chapter 6, Khallouk (2025)'s synthesis situates these case-based experiments within the UAE's broader Vision 2031 and Digital Economy Strategy, positioning Smart IS adoption as an entrepreneurial driver of sustainable diversification. The *Playbook* therefore not only reflects applied research outcomes but also offers a roadmap for policymakers, educators, and SMEs seeking to align innovation with national digital priorities.

7.1. Reinforcing the Core Principles

1. **Integration precedes innovation**: Cohesive systems and aligned processes form the foundation for meaningful innovation, as demonstrated by the CRM transformation cases that centralized customer data and automated workflows before layering advanced analytics.
2. **Sustainability must be measurable**: Impact must be tracked, quantified, and communicated through digital dashboards and KPIs, ensuring transparency and accountability in achieving environmental and social goals.
3. **Ecosystem partnerships accelerate growth**: Collaboration across suppliers, customers, regulators, and academic institutions enables resource sharing, market access, and innovation at scale, turning digital transformation into a collective enterprise rather than an isolated effort.

These three principles collectively form the foundation of a unified framework for future-proofing SMEs through Smart IS adoption. The framework (Figure 1) illustrates how integration, measurable sustainability, and ecosystem collaboration align with the roles of SMEs, policymakers, and academia to generate shared outcomes, that is, resilience, competitiveness, and sustainable growth.

This model illustrates how the three core principles - Integration Precedes Innovation, Sustainability Must Be Measurable, and Ecosystem Partnerships Accelerate Growth - interconnect with key stakeholders. Through their collective actions, SMEs, policymakers, and academia contribute to building resilient, competitive, and sustainable enterprises within the UAE's digital economy.

Ultimately, this *Playbook* serves not only as a compilation of academic insights but also as a practical guide and source of inspiration for entrepreneurs, policymakers, and educators. It highlights that future-proofing businesses in the era of digital convergence requires integrated, human-centered, and data-driven strategies that balance operational excellence, market responsiveness, and sustainability.

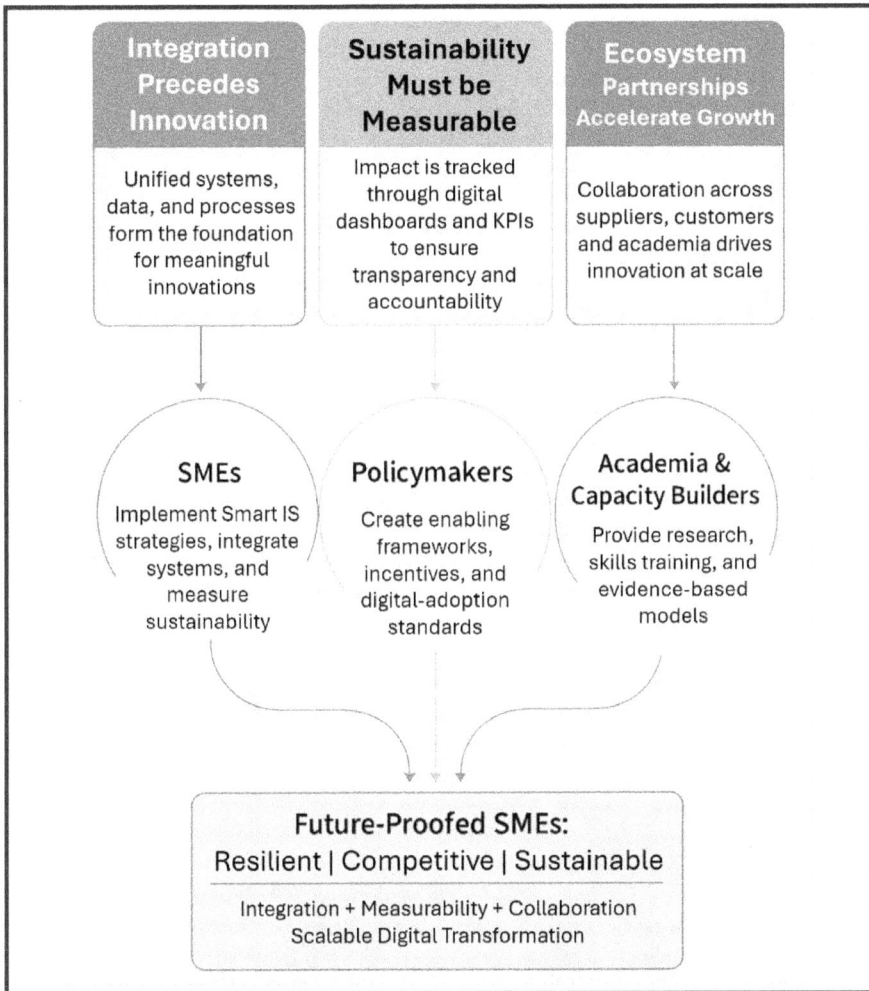

Figure 2: Framework for Future-Proofing SMEs through Smart Information Systems

8. Call to Action

> **For Entrepreneurs**: Adopt Smart IS and emerging technologies strategically, fostering innovation while embedding sustainability into your business models. Prioritize integration and interoperability before expanding into more advanced CRM tools. Look for

measurable ROI through digital sustainability metrics.

For Policymakers: Develop supportive frameworks, incentives, and collaborative platforms to accelerate SME digital adoption. Design frameworks that incentivize SMEs to adopt integrated CRM ecosystems and measure sustainable impact.

For Academics and Capacity Builders: Strengthen project-based learning, ap- plied research, and curricula that equip future business leaders with the skills and mindset to navigate the digital era. Conduct further research on the impact of digital maturity on CRM adoption, particularly in developing regions.

By embracing these principles and lessons, SMEs can position themselves not only to survive today's challenges but to thrive and lead in the digital economies of tomorrow. Ultimately, this *Playbook* illustrates how empowering students as applied researchers can bridge academic insight and enterprise innovation. The collective findings reaffirm that responsible technology adoption, grounded in ethics, sustainability, and collaboration, will define the next decade of SME transformation across the UAE and beyond.

9. References

Ali, M., Khan, T. I., Khattak, M. N., & Şener, İ. (2024). Synergizing AI and business: Maximizing innovation. *Journal of Business Innovation and Technology*. https://doi.org/10.1016/j.joitmc.2024.100352

Amosu, O.R., Kumar, P., Ogunsuji, Y. M., *et al.* (2024). AI-driven demand forecasting: Enhancing inventory management and customer satisfaction. *World Journal of Advanced Research and Reviews*, 23(2), 100–110. https://doi.org/10.30574/wjarr.2024.23.2.2394

Awad, J. A. R., & Martín-Rojas, R. (2024). Digital transformation influence on organisational resilience through organisational learning and innovation. *Journal of Innovation and Entrepreneurship*, *13*, 69. https://doi.org/10.1186/s13731-024-00405-4

da Silva, A., de Almeida, I.D., Dionisio, A. *et al.* (2025) How digital technologies enhance competitiveness in manufacturing

SMEs. *J Innov Entrep* **14**, 103 (2025). https://doi.org/10.1186/s13731-025-00576-8

European Parliament & Council. (2016). Regulation (EU) 2016/679 of the European Parliament and of the Council of 27 April 2016 on the protection of natural persons with regard to the processing of personal data and on the free movement of such data (General Data Protection Regulation). *Official Journal of the European Union, L119*, 1–88. https://eur-lex.europa.eu/legal-content/EN/TXT/?uri=CELEX%3A32016R0679

Franzè, C., Paolucci, E., & Pessot, E. (2024). *Sustained value creation driven by digital connectivity: A multiple case study in the mechanical components industry. Technovation, 129*, 102918. https://doi.org/10.1016/j.technovation.2023.102918

Frempong, D., Akinboboye, O., Okoli, I., Afrihiya, E., & Omei, M. (2022). Real-time analytics dashboards for decision-making using Tableau in public sector and business intelligence applications. *Journal of Frontiers in Multidisciplinary Research, 3*(2), 65–80. 10.54660/.IJFMR.2022.3.2.65-80

Geissdoerfer, M., Savaget, P., Bocken, N. M. P., & Hultink, E. J (2017). The circular economy — A new sustainability paradigm? *Journal of Cleaner Production*, 143, 757–768. https://doi.org/10.1016/j.jclepro.2016.12.048

Hafeez, S., Shahzad, K., & De Silva, M. (2025). Enhancing digital transformation in SMEs: The dynamic capabilities of innovation intermediaries within ecosystems. *Long Range Planning, 58*(3), 102525. https://doi.org/10.1016/j.lrp.2025.102525

Hristov, I., & Chirico, A. (2019). The Role of Sustainability Key Performance Indicators (KPIs) in Implementing Sustainable Strategies. *Sustainability, 11*(20), 5742. https://doi.org/10.3390/su11205742

Hussain, T. S., Kumar, A. A., & Elgamil, M. (2025). Building a Conscious Commerce Engine: A Smart IS Framework for a UAE-based eco-friendly fashion marketplace. In Z. R. Khan, P. Bhagwat, P. Mukala, & N. Ruxwana (Eds.), *Technology adoption playbook for sustainability-focused startups and SMEs* (pp. 61-77). ENAI WG Centre for Academic Integrity in the UAE; University of Wollongong in Dubai; Gulf Book Services LTD, UK.

ISO - International Organization for Standardization. (2022). *ISO/IEC 27001:2022 — Information security management systems*. ISO. https://www.iso.org/standard/27001

Kallmuenzer, A., Mikhaylov, A., Chelaru, M. *et al.* (2025) Adoption and performance outcome of digitalization in small and medium-sized enterprises. *Rev Manag Sci* **19**, 2011–2038 (2025). https://doi.org/10.1007/s11846-024-00744-2

Khan, I. (2025). *Undisrupted: Leadership essentials on business transformation, profitability, and future readiness.* John Wiley & Sons. ISBN: 978-1-394-21582-9

Khallouk, M (2025). Connecting the Dots: Innovation, Entrepreneurship, and the Sustainable Future. In Z. R. Khan, P. Bhagwat, P. Mukala, & N. Ruxwana (Eds.), *Technology adoption playbook for sustainability-focused startups and SMEs* (pp. 111-122). ENAI WG Centre for Academic Integrity in the UAE; University of Wollongong in Dubai; Gulf Book Services LTD, UK

Kolawole, F., (2023). AI-Powered Customer Insights: Enhancing SME Marketing Strategies (March 10, 2023). Available at SSRN: https://ssrn.com/abstract=5139655 or http://dx.doi.org/10.2139/ssrn.5139655

Li, J. (2025). Challenges and strategies for SMEs in the apparel industry: Navigating technological and sustainable transformations. *In Proceedings of the 1st International Conference on Modern Logistics and Supply Chain Management (MLSCM 2024),* 457-460 ISBN: 978-989-758-738-2
https://www.scitepress.org/Papers/2024/133379/133379.pdf

Ma, D., & Zhu, Q. (2022). Innovation in emerging economies: Research on the digital economy driving high-quality green development. *Journal of Business Research, 145,* 801–813. https://doi.org/10.1016/j.jbusres.2022.03.041

McKinsey (2017). Smartening up with artificial intelligence: How AI will transform Germany's industrial sector. McKinsey & Company. https://www.mckinsey.com/industries/semiconductors/our-insights/smartening-up-with-artificial-intelligence

McKinsey (2024). Rewired and running ahead: Digital and AI leaders are leaving the rest behind. https://www.mckinsey.com/capabilities/mckinsey-digital/our-insights/rewired-and-running-ahead-digital-and-ai-leaders-are-leaving-the-rest-behind

Melo, I. C., Queiroz, G. A., Alves Junior, *et al.* (2023). Sustainable digital transformation in small and medium enterprises (SMEs): A review on performance. *Heliyon, 9*(3), e13908. https://doi.org/10.1016/j.heliyon.2023.e13908

NIST (2024). The NIST Cybersecurity Framework (CSF) 2.0. National Institute of Standards and Technology. https://nvlpubs.nist.gov/nistpubs/CSWP/NIST.CSWP.29.pdf

Noronha, N., Dypiangco, R.., D'souza, F., & Mathew, N (2025). Next-Gen CRMs for SMEs: Enhancing Customer Engagement with RAP Plugins. In Z. R. Khan, P. Bhagwat, P. Mukala, & N. Ruxwana (Eds.), *Technology adoption playbook for sustainability-focused startups and SMEs* (pp. 81-95). ENAI WG Centre for Academic Integrity in the UAE; University of Wollongong in Dubai; Gulf Book Services LTD, UK.

OECD (2021). *The Digital Transformation of SMEs*. Paris: OECD Publishing. https://www.oecd.org/en/publications/the-digital-transformation-of-smes_bdb9256a-en.html

OECD. (2024). *SME digitalisation to manage shocks and transitions: 2024 OECD D4SME survey*. OECD Publishing. https://doi.org/10.1787/eb4ec9ac-en

Omand, D. (2023). *How to Survive a Crisis: Lessons in Resilience and Avoiding Disaster*. Penguin/Viking. https://cdn.penguin.co.uk/dam-assets/books/9780241561331/9780241561331-sample.pdf

Ranjbar, S., Islam, F., & Virani, H. (2025). Enabling Business Intelligence through Unified CRM Ecosystems. In Z. R. Khan, P. Bhagwat, P. Mukala, & N. Ruxwana (Eds.), *Technology adoption playbook for sustainability-focused startups and SMEs* (pp. 97-108). ENAI WG Centre for Academic Integrity in the UAE; University of Wollongong in Dubai; Gulf Book Services LTD, UK.

Romero, I., & Mammadov, H. (2025) Digital Transformation of Small and Medium-Sized Enterprises as an Innovation Process: A Holistic Study of its Determinants. *J Knowl Econ* 16, 8496–8523 (2025). https://doi.org/10.1007/s13132-024-02217-z

Sagala, G. H., & Őri, D. (2024). Exploring digital transformation strategy to achieve SMEs resilience and antifragility: a systematic literature review. *Journal of Small Business & Entrepreneurship*, 37(3), 495–524. https://doi.org/10.1080/08276331.2024.2392080

Shaikh, A. N., Sujith, A., Bikram, R. S., & Roy, A. (2025). Empowering Sustainable Growth with Smart IS – The Fashion SME. In Z. R. Khan, P. Bhagwat, P. Mukala, & N. Ruxwana (Eds.), *Technology adoption playbook for sustainability-focused startups and SMEs* (pp. 27-40). ENAI WG Centre for Academic Integrity in the UAE; University of Wollongong in Dubai; Gulf Book Services LTD, UK.

Sudirman, I. D., Astuty, E., & Aryanto, R. (2025). Enhancing Digital Technology Adoption in SMEs Through Sustainable Resilience Strategy: Examining the Role of Entrepreneurial Orientation and Competencies. *Journal of Small Business Strategy*, 35(1), 97–114. https://doi.org/10.53703/001c.124907

Tauro, A. N., Varughese, A., Sapavat, A. S. & Arar, L. (2025). Intelligent & Sustainable Supply Chain for Smart Retail. In Z. R. Khan, P. Bhagwat, P. Mukala, & N. Ruxwana (Eds.), *Technology adoption playbook for sustainability-focused startups and SMEs* (pp. 43-58). ENAI WG Centre for Academic Integrity in the UAE; University of Wollongong in Dubai; Gulf Book Services LTD, UK.

Yang, G., Li, H., Nie, Y., Yue, Z., & Wang, H. (2023). Digital transformation and firm performance: the role of factor allocation. *Applied Economics, 56*(50), 6203–6220. https://doi.org/10.1080/00036846.2023.2269631 https://doi.org/10.1080/00036846.2023.2269631

UAE Digital Government (2023). UAE Digital Government Strategy 2025. https://u.ae/en/about-the-uae/strategies-initiatives-and-awards/strategies-plans-and-visions/government-services-and-digital-transformation/uae-national-digital-government-strategy

UAE Government (2024). We the UAE 2031 vision. https://u.ae/en/about-the-uae/strategies-initiatives-and-awards/strategies-plans-and-visions/innovation-and-future-shaping/we-the-uae-2031-vision

United Nations (2015). Transforming our world: The 2030 Agenda for Sustainable Development (A/RES/70/1). https://sdgs.un.org/2030agenda

Wang, S., & Zhang, H. (2025). *Enhancing SMEs' sustainable innovation and performance through digital transformation: Insights from strategic technology, organizational dynamics, and environmental adaptation. Socio-Economic Planning Sciences, 98,* 102124. https://doi.org/10.1016/j.seps.2024.102124

Wedel, M. & Kamakura, W.A. (2000). *Market segmentation: Conceptual and methodological foundations.* Springer, Boston, MA. https://doi.org/10.1007/978-1-4615-4651-1

Wei, J., & Shen, Y. (2025). Impact and mechanism of digital transformation on performance in manufacturing firms. *Innovation and Green Development, 4*(1), 100205. https://doi.org/10.1016/j.igd.2025.100205

World Bank (2019–ongoing). Small and Medium Enterprises (SMEs) Finance (overview). https://www.worldbank.org/en/topic/smefinance

Acknowledgements

This book would not have been possible without the generous support, encouragement, and contributions of many individuals and institutions.
We are deeply grateful to the University of Wollongong in Dubai for providing a vibrant academic environment where students and faculty alike are encouraged to experiment, innovate, and share knowledge. We extend our sincere thanks to our President, Professor Mohamed Salem, for his unwavering vision and leadership, and to Professor Mai El Barachi, Head of School of Computer Science, whose guidance and dedication have been a constant source of strength.

We wish to acknowledge Professor Farhad Oroumchian, Program Leader for General Computer Science whose encouragement of this work and longstanding commitment to mentoring students has elevated the quality of our outcomes. We also extend our heartfelt thanks to the national and international reviewers, including esteemed colleagues within UOWD, who generously offered their time and expertise to provide valuable feedback and guidance to both students and editors. As this book features student-authored chapters, the review process followed a mentor-review model rather than a traditional blind peer review, with reviewers fully informed of the book's goals and educational premise. Their thoughtful insights greatly enhanced the clarity, depth, and academic rigor of the final work.

Our appreciation also goes to the many WISP mentors, who have volunteered their time and expertise year after year to nurture student learning and industry engagement.

We are also indebted to the ENAI Working Group Centre for Academic Integrity in the UAE, ZAISH, and our network of supporters who have championed this project from its inception. A special word of thanks goes to our alumnus, Mr. Mohamad Hammad, whose encouragement exemplifies the enduring relationship between our graduates and the university.

Finally, we acknowledge the countless family members, friends, colleagues, and well-wishers in the lives of our student authors and editors. Their patience, encouragement, and belief carried us through the long and sometimes gruelling months of developing this manuscript. To all of you, we offer our heartfelt gratitude.

Zeenath Reza Khan
Pradnya Bhagwat
Patrick Mukala
Nkqubela Ruxwana

Declarations

Informed Consents and Ethics
The chapters in this playbook are not about any single company. Instead, they draw on generalised SME pain points observed across multiple student-led explorations. All examples have been anonymised and abstracted, ensuring no individual company is described or represented.
The focus is on recurring challenges faced by SMEs in the UAE and the creative solutions students envisioned in response. These insights are presented as practical, thematic guidance for the wider SME community, rather than case studies of specific firms.

Conflict of Interest Statement
The editors and contributors declare that there are no conflicts of interest. Company partners provided informed consent to participate in student learning activities during work-integrated learning experiences in various subjects, and all examples in this playbook are anonymised and presented thematically to ensure confidentiality.

Funding sources
This playbook was supported by the ENAI Working Group Centre for Academic Integrity in the UAE, with additional contributions from Zaish and UOWD alumnus Mr. Mohamad Hamad. Their support made it possible to develop and publish this resource as a practical guide for SMEs, readily available to the wider community as print-to-order and in an open-access spirit. To ensure global reach and ease of distribution, it is published at a nominal server charge of USD 1/- only. This approach reflects our commitment to knowledge-sharing while covering the minimal hosting costs of digital platforms Importantly, all funding sources were strictly supportive in nature and did not influence the content, analysis, or recommendations presented in this work. This approach reflects our ongoing commitment to transparency, academic independence, and equitable knowledge-sharing.

Data availability
This playbook does not contain or rely on proprietary company data. The content is based on anonymised and generalised insights drawn from applied learning activities in Information Systems courses. As such, no underlying datasets are available for sharing, and all company and student information remains confidential.

Editors

Zeenath Reza Khan is an Associate Professor of Responsible Information Systems and a leading voice in AI ethics and academic integrity. She was among the first recipients of the Dubai Future Foundation Research Grant for AI trustworthiness in healthcare and education. Founder of the ENAI WG Centre for Academic Integrity in the UAE, she has authored key works including *Ethics of AI in Academia.* Her IEPAR framework and innovative teaching practices integrate generative AI responsibly into classrooms worldwide. She is a recipient of the 2024 Tracey Bretag Academic Integrity Award and the Al Safeer Ambassador Award (Dubai DET).

Pradnya Bhagwat serves as an Instructor in the School of Computer Science at the University of Wollongong in Dubai. She holds a Master's degree in Telecommunications and Software Engineering. Pradnya is a passionate and results-driven Software Engineer with over 15 years of experience across diverse roles and geographies, including the United States and the Middle East. Her professional journey has taken her through some of the world's most respected organizations - Motorola, Nokia, Expedia, and Wells Fargo. Her primary competencies are project management using Agile and Scrum, Software Quality Assurance and Automation. At UOWD, Pradnya currently focuses on teaching Business Information Systems courses. In this academic role, Pradnya brings industry insights into the classroom, designing interactive lab sessions, crafting practical assignments, and mentoring students to think critically and apply theoretical knowledge to real-world challenges. Pradnya is passionate about learning and has completed multiple certifications with IBM, ISTQB, Six Sigma and recently an online certification in Big Data Engineering.

Patrick Mukala is an Assistant Professor of Artificial Intelligence and Data Science with a double PhD in Computer Science. His teaching philosophy places students at the centre of learning, combining practical applications with theory to ensure relevance and impact. His research focuses on eXplainable, Ethical, and Trustworthy AI, Algorithm Engineering, and Applied Analytics across learning, healthcare, and governance contexts. He has extensive experience in semantic web, abstract state machines, and automata theory, and has taught and researched in South Africa and the Netherlands. Before academia, he worked over five years in industry roles in data architecture, engineering, and AI.

Nkqubela Ruxwana is an accomplished academic and seasoned IT professional with expertise in digital transformation, complex IT solutions implementation, and cybersecurity with a focus on governance, risk, and compliance (GRC). In his academic capacity, he has led research teams, supervised postgraduate theses, and published across diverse ICT domains. His research interests include digital transformation, cybersecurity, information systems adoption theories, cloud computing, eHealth, and ICT4D. Beyond academia, he has held technical and senior management roles with organisations such as Telkom, Vodacom, and Nedbank, helping design ICT strategies, strengthen cybersecurity, and drive digital transformation initiatives. He has received several awards for research and professional excellence, holds multiple professional certifications, and is an active member of professional associations in IT and cybersecurity

Review and Advisory Board

Farhad Oroumchian is a distinguished academic and researcher with extensive international experience in the United States, Iran, and the UAE. Prior to joining UOWD, he served as Chair of Software Engineering at the University of Tehran and held senior engineering and consulting roles in New York. His expertise spans information retrieval, natural language processing, multilingual search engines, and Persian text processing, including the development of an intelligent search engine that uses human-like reasoning. Prof. Oroumchian has published over 100 papers, with his research cited more than 1,000 times worldwide.

Kamal Jaafar is an accomplished individual with a strong academic background and extensive experience in the field of engineering. Having earned both an MPhil and a PhD degree from Cambridge University (UK), he has been recognized for his scholarly achievements by being honored as a fellow of the Cambridge Overseas Trust by King Charles. In addition to his academic pursuits, Dr. Jaafar is a seasoned project management consultant, having worked with prestigious multinational corporations such as China Petroleum (CPECC), Abu Dhabi National Oil and Gas Company (ANOC), and Kuwait Oil Corporation (KOC). Dr. Jaafar's expertise is not confined to the corporate world; he is also a published author, with his notable work, "Digital Transformation of Project Management," published by Taylor and Francis, showcasing his thought leadership in the field

Mohamad Nassereddine is an Assistant Professor at the University of Wollongong in Dubai, specializing in renewable energy, smart power systems, high-voltage transmission, substations, and advanced smart grids. With over 13 years of industry experience in the design, management, and commissioning of complex power networks, he brings real-world expertise to his teaching. His research focuses on sustainable power systems and innovation in energy infrastructure. Dr. Nassereddine earned his PhD, Master of Engineering (Hons), and Bachelor of Engineering from Western Sydney University, Australia. He received the "Outstanding Project Energy Manager of the Year Award" at the International Sustainable Government Housing event in 2019.

Thomas Lancaster is a Senior Fellow of the Higher Education Academy, and Senior Teaching Fellow - Computing at Imperial College London UK. With a PhD from London South Bank University in plagiarism detection, he has served as Associate Dean for Recruitment at Staffordshire University and held senior roles at Coventry and Birmingham City Universities. His work bridges computing education, employability, and integrity, and he has delivered keynotes and training worldwide.

Faculty Author

Marouane Khallouk is an Assistant Professor of Innovation and Entrepreneurship at the University of Wollongong in Dubai. He forged strong collaborations with leading institutions such as the Dubai Future Foundation and Dubai SME, where his students secure grants, gain access to accelerator programs, and achieve recognition, including one mentee who was named Best Student Entrepreneur in the UAE. As co-organizer of the UOWD Entrepreneurship Fair, he has engaged over 370 students and 30 teams, with winners receiving one-year incubation, funding opportunities, and a place in the Startup World Cup. His innovative course designs and large-scale blended learning initiatives have earned both an Innovation Award for digital engagement and a Collaboration Award for international cross-campus impact.

Student Authors

Aagna Samhita Sapavat is a final-year Computer Science student at the University of Wollongong in Dubai, specializing in Big Data and Artificial Intelligence. She has hands-on experience in Python-based machine learning and deep learning, with projects such as Bitcoin price prediction and data-driven analysis. Through industry exposure, she has strengthened her expertise in building and tracking ML models with MLflow, alongside translating technical insights into business value. Aagna also brings creativity to her technical work, designing interactive dashboards in Power BI, intuitive prototypes in Figma, and visual narratives in Canva. Her academic and project portfolio covers systems development, secure web applications, and UI/UX design, showcasing her versatility across engineering and design. A confident speaker and team player, she is passionate about creating AI solutions that are technically robust, user-centric, and business-driven.

Abel Varughese is a final-year Computer Science student specializing in Big Data and Artificial Intelligence. He has developed strong skills in Python, MySQL, C++, and web technologies, with hands-on experience in building applications and working on both individual and team-based projects. Passionate about harnessing modern technologies and AI to address complex challenges, he combines technical expertise with adaptability and creativity. Beyond academics, Abel has gained work experience in AI and Cloud Security, participated in business and innovation competitions, and actively engaged in leadership-focused activities, further strengthening his problem-solving, communication, and teamwork abilities.

Advaith Sujith is a researcher in Artificial Intelligence (AI) and Data Science, with a focus on statistical patterns and their applications in AI. He has published work on Zipf's Law and its relevance to large language models (LLMs), and has also contributed to award-winning AI projects in applied settings. He is currently pursuing a Master's in Machine Learning at the University of Manchester, where he bridges rigorous research with curiosity-driven exploration of AI's potential in real-world contexts.

150

Akhil Anil Kumar is a Computer Science graduate working as a Product Owner in the AI team at one.com, where he focuses on developing consumer applications and enhancing user experience. He previously helped establish a startup called Volume Stories, contributing to product design and early growth initiatives. His interests lie at the intersection of design and technology, combining technical skills with user-centred thinking to create practical, impactful solutions.

Anushka Roy is a recent Computer Science graduate specializing in Artificial Intelligence and Big Data, with a strong background in data science and machine learning. She has grown her expertise by developing and optimizing models for practical applications, demonstrated through her success in academic projects and hackathons aimed at solving real-world challenges. With a solid foundation in predictive analytics, deep learning, and distributed data computing, she is dedicated to building AI systems that are not only innovative and high-performing but also ethical. Her aim is to contribute to cross-functional R&D teams focused on creating intelligent, data-informed products that address evolving industry needs.

Ashton Vivian Tauro is a final-year Computer Science student at the University of Wollongong in Dubai, specializing in Artificial Intelligence and Big Data. He has worked on projects including an AI-based taxi demand forecasting system, a multilingual AI voice translator, and full-stack platforms. His academic and hackathon experiences have sharpened his skills in AI/ML, coding, data science, and system analysis, while building strong teamwork and problem-solving abilities. Versatile and adaptable, Ashton approaches challenges from both technical and user-focused perspectives, delivering practical and creative solutions. Beyond academics, he draws inspiration from music and art, often sparking innovative ideas for his work. Passionate about blending technology with creativity, he strives to design solutions that are robust, user-centric, and impactful.

Asraa Noohu Shaikh is a recent BSc Computer Science graduate specializing in Artificial Intelligence and Big Data, who is currently applying her expertise in AI and machine learning at a Multinational Corporation. With a strong passion for Mathematics, she thrives in developing intelligent systems and leveraging data-driven problem-solving. She is highly proficient in Python. Her specific expertise includes machine learning algorithms, deep learning, and advanced data analysis, which she applies to extract insights from complex datasets by utilizing mathematical and statistical concepts. She has also demonstrated innovation and leadership by winning Hackathons and serving as an Executive for the UOWD Women in STEM society. She is dedicated to driving impactful AI projects and collaborating on innovative solutions within the tech industry.

Farhana Islam is a final-year Computer Science student with a strong foundation in both technical skills and creative problem-solving. She has explored areas such as UI/UX design, AI, cybersecurity, app development, frontend development, and business technology. Over the course of her studies, she has contributed to a variety of projects that showcase her technical abilities and innovative mindset, strengthening her coding expertise while broadening her perspective on real-world applications. Farhana is driven by complex challenges and applies a blend of user-focused design and strategic problem-solving to deliver solutions with meaningful impact.

Frenica D'Souza is specializing in Big Data and Artificial Intelligence while pursuing a Bachelor of Computer Science at the University of Wollongong, Dubai. She has gained experience through diverse projects, including game development, dynamic web applications, data-driven systems, and blockchain-based solutions. She demonstrates both technical and creative problem-solving abilities, with a strong foundation in data analysis and software development. Over the summer, she interned as a Data Analyst cum Software Developer, further enhancing her practical knowledge. She brings a passion for innovation, analytical thinking, and user-centered design to her academic and professional pursuits.

Hawra Virani is a recent Computer Science graduate with a specialization in Artificial Intelligence and Big Data. She has developed expertise in handling large-scale datasets, statistical analysis, predictive modeling, and machine learning, combining technical knowledge with problem-solving skills. Through academic and practical projects, she has applied data-driven approaches to uncover insights, optimize processes, and address real-world challenges. Passionate about innovation, she is committed to leveraging technology, AI techniques, and advanced analytics to support smarter decision-making and contribute to impactful digital transformation initiatives.

Loulieh Anas Arar is a final-year Business and Information Systems student who thrives at the intersection of technology, business, and human-centric design. She is driven by a passion for creating solutions that are not only technically sound but also deliver meaningful user and business value. Her work on various academic projects has strengthened her skills in systems analysis, UX-informed design, and data-driven decision making. Versatile and adaptable, Loulieh enjoys collaborative environments where she can leverage her unique BIS perspective to solve complex problems. She is curious, innovative, and dedicated to applying her interdisciplinary skills to build efficient and intuitive digital solutions.

Maryam Elgamil is a final-year Business Information Systems (BIS) student at the University of Wollongong of Dubai, with a strong interest in management, innovation, and technology. Building on her family business background, she is pursuing a business-oriented path that combines practical experience with academic learning. Maryam has earned recognition through multiple competitions, including Injaz and NSTI with the Ministry of Education in the United Arab Emirates. These achievements have strengthened her leadership, collaboration, and problem-solving skills while fostering an entrepreneurial mindset. She is passionate about applying digital solutions and business strategies to drive sustainable growth and create a meaningful impact.

153

Nathan Mathew is a motivated student currently pursuing a Bachelor of Business Information Systems at the University of Wollongong in Dubai. With a strong interest in technology, data, and innovation, he enjoys exploring how digital tools can improve transparency, efficiency, and everyday experiences. He has worked on projects ranging from smart city applications and rental property management systems to customer sentiment analysis tools. He is currently interning with ASMAK as an IT Intern, where he is gaining hands-on industry experience. Curious and adaptable, he is driven by a desire to connect technology with real-world solutions and is preparing to build a career where business and technology meet.

Nigel Noronha is an AI Engineer at Solutions+, where he builds automation systems that streamline HR, finance, and procurement operations across large-scale government and enterprise environments. He previously contributed to internal tooling and product innovation at MCG Talent and has explored side projects in recruitment automation and content systems. With a background in software engineering and experience deploying no-code tools like n8n in production, Nigel focuses on solving real-world problems through efficient, scalable AI infrastructure.

Raphael Dypiangco is a fourth year student at the University of Wollongong in Dubai, pursuing a Bachelor's degree in Business Information Systems (BIS). With a strong interest in the intersection of business and technology, he has gained hands-on experience in auditing company operations and developing innovative digital solutions. Notably, he contributed to the proposal of a modular Customer Relationship Management (CRM) system designed to enhance organizational efficiency and adaptability. Raphael is passionate about leveraging information systems to improve business decision-making and drive digital transformation in modern enterprises.

Rhythm Bikram Shahi is a Machine Learning and AI specialist with a strong background in UI/UX design, graphic design, and photography. A graduate of the University of Wollongong in Dubai, he has contributed to several award-winning projects, including automated crypto trading systems, disease detection models, and AI accessibility tools. He has collaborated with organizations and innovators worldwide, helping them develop AI-powered solutions that drive smart growth. As a team leader, Rhythm balances discipline with a sharp eye for detail, ensuring that every solution and report meets the highest standards. His creativity enhances his technical expertise, enabling him to design intuitive and visually appealing user interfaces. Committed and ambitious, he aims to use technology to create meaningful change.

Sara Ranjbar is a final-year Computer Science student with a strong focus on collaboration, creativity, and critical thinking. She is passionate about UI/UX design, app and frontend development, as well as AI and cybersecurity. Throughout her studies, she has worked on diverse projects that highlight both technical expertise and design thinking, strengthening her programming skills and fostering innovation. She enjoys tackling challenges that push boundaries, applying user-centered thinking and problem-solving to develop digital solutions that make a meaningful impact.

Taha Shabbir Hussain is a Computer Science graduate specializing in Artificial Intelligence and Data Analytics, combining strong technical skills with strategic insight. He has delivered impactful AI solutions for government entities, including an award-winning citizen engagement platform for Fujairah Municipality recognized at GITEX. He also developed an AI-powered voice tutor for visually impaired learners with Samsung Innovation Campus. As a community builder, he grew a network of over 1,000 technology enthusiasts, collaborating with Binance, the Ministry of Tolerance, and GITEX, earning Best Club of the Year. Co-founding CyberNova, he leads blockchain research on zero-knowledge verification and regularly speaks at major technology conferences. Driven and recognized with the Most Dedicated Student Award, Taha aims to build data-driven solutions with lasting social impact

ZAISH

European Network
for Academic Integrity
Outreach Working Group

CENTRE FOR
ACADEMIC INTEGRITY
IN THE UAE

www.ingramcontent.com/pod-product-compliance
Lightning Source LLC
Chambersburg PA
CBHW070930210326
41520CB00021B/6876